RELAP

HOW TO AVOID OR ESCAPE THEM

by

ROBERT D. RAMSEY Ed.D.

FIRST EDITION

Newjoy Press
Ventura California USA

Relapse Traps
How to Avoid or Escape Them

Robert D. Ramsey Ed.D.

Published by:
Newjoy Press
Post Office Box 3437
Ventura, California 93006-3437 USA

Cataloging in Publication Data
Ramsey, Robert D.
    Relapse Traps: How to Avoid or Escape Them by Robert D. Ramsey Ed.D - first edition
Includes bibliographical references
ISBN 1-879899-00-0
1. Addiction Treatment
2. Relapse Prevention
3. Alcoholism Treatment
4. Treatment, Alcoholism

Library of Congress No. 98-065294
ISBN 1-879899-00-0 $15.95

Dedication

To 7-HI AA and
River Ridge Treatment Center

My personal resources for recovery

The Table of Contents

About the Author

Dr. Robert D. Ramsey is a lifelong educator and free lance writer from Minneapolis. He is also a recovering alcoholic and an active member of Alcoholics Anonymous. In this latter role, he has served as an Advisory Board member for a leading chemical dependency treatment center in the Twin Cities.

Dr. Ramsey's publications include *501 Ways to Boost Your Child's Self Esteem* and *Mother's Wisdom* (Contemporary Books).

Through his writings, Dr. Ramsey has helped thousands of parents, teachers and students to improve their lives. His latest work, *Relapse Traps*, can do the same for all those alcoholics who want to feel better, live better, stay sober and remain relapse free!

Disclaimer

This book is designed to provide information concerning the subject matter covered. It is sold with the understanding that neither the publisher nor the author are engaged in rendering therapy or other professional services through this book.

Every effort has been made to make this book as complete and accurate as possible. However, there may be mistakes, both typographical and in content. Therefore, this text should only be used as a general guide and not as the ultimate source of relapse prevention information.

The purpose of this book is to educate and entertain. The author and Newjoy Press shall have neither liability nor responsibility to any person or entity with respect to any loss or damage caused, or alleged to be caused, directly or indirectly by the information in this book.

If you do not wish to be bound by the above, you may return this book to the publisher for a full refund.

Introduction

USER'S MANUAL

"There are only two times when you are liable to relapse: when you are alone and when you are with somebody." Anon.

Relapse is a ghost that haunts all recovering alcoholics. At least 50% of alcoholics (and 60% to 80% of other addicts) who receive treatment experience a relapse. Relapse often occurs during the first year but it can happen anytime during recovery–even after years of successful sobriety.

Obviously then, every alcoholic who wants to stop drinking and stay sober must be concerned about the risk of relapse.

Any relapse is a setback but some are more serious than others. A relapse can even lead to suicidal behavior. The good news is that most relapses don't have to happen. Although they are common, relapses are avoidable and preventable.

Even chronic alcoholics with a long history of failed recovery can learn to escape relapses. Prevention requires self-awareness and carefully planned action. The secret is to get around the everyday traps that frequently trigger backsliding incidents.

No one can make you drink; no one can make you stop; and no one can keep you from sliding into relapse. You must do it yourself. However, you don't have to do it alone. Help is available. It's as close as the book you are reading.

Relapse Traps is a one-of-a-kind, hands on, stay-sober tool for recovering alcoholics. This practical, action guide identifies 65 of the most common triggers that regularly cause slips and relapses.

What is more important, it pinpoints customized action plans to avoid or escape each of these familiar traps. Each section is filled with life-tested emergency measure that can be used to build your own coping plans to resist relapses.

Taken as a whole, this handbook provides a well-rounded crash course in relapse prevention. However, a better use is to use the book as a reference. You will find specific steps to enable you to handle everyday situations such as the traps in family, work, social life, physical problems, mental/emotional issues and attitude that often sidetrack sobriety. Think of *Relapse Traps* as lifesaving first aid for any alcoholic's endangered recovery.

Besides the 65 sets of proven, relapse prevention strategies, this manual includes a variety of special, sobriety saving aids such as:

- ▸ Warning signs. (Signals of a relapse just waiting to happen.)
- ▸ How to say, "No." (Ways to turn down a drink and make it stick.)
- ▸ Alcohol-free fun. (How to have a life and enjoy it–without drinking.)
- ▸ Self-Talk (Self-affirmations that help prevent relapse.)
- ▸ Personal pampering. (Ways to reward yourself for averting relapse.)
- ▸ A relapse prevention reading list.

With all of these user-friendly coping tools, *Relapse Traps* is a powerful and comprehensive relapse prevention resource that really works. It can be used over and over as a defense against life's daily assaults on fragile sobriety. This unusual self-help guide belongs on the book shelves of all alcoholics commited to recovery and those who want to help them sustain it.

Recovery is too precious to risk losing through relapse. Fortunately, preparation and precaution can defuse most potential threats to sobriety. You can learn to live virtually relapse free. Why not gain the proactive advantage of using this guide's proven relapse resistors?

Allow the realistic tips and suggestions throughout the book to make up your personal prescription for lasting recovery. Take as much and as often as needed. You can't overdose on good advice.

SECTION I

FAMILY TRAPS

1

Section I

FAMILY TRAPS

Life begins and ends with family. Often, so does alcoholism. For many sufferers, problems with alcohol abuse are rooted in childhood experiences, parental attitudes, family expectations and/or the pressures of family responsibilities.

Dysfunctional families produce dysfunctional individuals–you may be one of them. Some families are physically or sexually abusive. Others make drinking a tradition. Some impose unreasonable demands. Many are almost impossible to please. For a variety of reasons, families generate more feelings of guilt and inadequacy than any other single source. Family problems and drinking problems often go hand-in-hand.

It's important to recognize the effect of family on sobriety. Constructing a family history can be useful in clarifying the role of family in your own patterns of alcohol use. However, it's not enough merely to see yourself as a victim. (This may even become just another excuse to drink.) What's needed is to get beyond victimization and to move on in building a sober life.

Sometimes, it starts by joining ACOA (Adult Children of Alcoholics) and/or involving family members in Alanon. Whatever it takes, lasting sobriety usually requires making peace with family or, at least, learning acceptance and forgiveness (of yourself and others).

It's no surprise that family factors not only contribute to many drinking problems in the first place, but are also frequent causes of relapses. Recovering alcoholics–especially those new to sobriety–are most vulnerable when around family members.

This section offers practical ways to deal with the most common family traps that trigger relapses and sabotage recovery. These action steps can help you reconnect with family one day at a time–without alcohol! If you can make it with your family, you can make it anywhere. Here's how.

Trap # 1 - Family Celebrations

Alcohol is often associated with family celebrations. Champagne is the beverage of choice at many birthdays, anniversaries and other special family gatherings. Toasting is a popular tradition in many families. Unfortunately, when booze is on the menu, relapse is a common visitor at family functions.

Family get-togethers are frequently filled with suppressed feelings and hidden agendas. It's no wonder many families fuel the warmth of their festivities with alcohol. Family celebrations are supposed to be fun but if you're trying to maintain a fragile, newly-won sobriety, they can be terrifying for many reasons:

► It's harder to turn down a drink from a family member than from anyone else.

► It's embarrassing to be the only nondrinker in a drinking family.

► It's threatening to admit addiction to parents or siblings who don't understand.

► It's difficult not to feel left out in a family that thinks alike and drinks alike.

All these actions are difficult but none are impossible. The secret is to have a plan and to stick with it no matter what. No one said recovery would be easy. Everyone says it's worth it!

Rejoining family celebrations is an important goal, but it's not worth a relapse and it doesn't have to be today. Don't participate if you feel intimidated. Why risk failure early on? Wait until you're ready. Then, choose the steps below which will help you most to cope with family celebrations without a slip.

Action Plan

▸ Talk to other recovering friends about how they handle family celebrations.

▸ Attend an AA meeting on the day of the celebration if possible.

▸ Rehearse your conversations in advance. Plan what to talk about.

▸ Show up after "happy hour."

▸ Take along a sober friend.

▸ Be realistic. Lower your expectations. No party or celebration is perfect.

▸ Follow the strategies that work for other kinds of parties (see Trap # 22).

▸ Stay only a short time if you're uncomfortable.

▸ Don't take that first drink. Ask for water instead.

▸ Remember whom you're not drinking for. (Clue: It's not your family.)

▸ Focus on what the family is really celebrating.

▸ Show you've changed. Act like the new person you

are.

▸ Use the occasion to atone for past indiscretions.

▸ Contribute something to the celebration (i.e., a favorite appetizer, a special dessert or an original centerpiece) to show your commitment to the family and the event.

▸ Make your sobriety part of the celebration. Ask others to share your relief and happiness.

Trap #2 - Family Holidays

All holidays are stressful. Holidays with families can be double whammies–especially for someone in early recovery. These events are like other family celebrations, only with the added pressures of living up to everyone's holiday expectations. Holidays magnify tensions. Tensions trigger cravings. Cravings are a slip waiting to happen.

Attending your first family holiday celebration sober is always a traumatic experience. You have too many memories; too many emotions; too much pain. Who needs a better reason to drink?

Handling family holidays during the early stages of recovery is tricky business. Sometimes, it's best to forego such celebrations until your foundation of sobriety is well established. If you decide to avoid the family at holiday time, it's important that you don't spend the time alone. Holidays + loneliness = self-pity and self-pity is a common precursor of relapse.

If necessary, create a temporary family of people you trust to help you get through the holiday. Spend time with those who are supportive, sober and fun. Seek out recovering friends, attend an AA meeting (or two) or volunteer to help at a homeless shelter. Whatever you do, don't do it alone. Holidays are people times. Don't be by yourself.

If you join in family holiday celebrations, focus on the real reason behind the holiday and keep in mind why it's important to be with family at these special times. Then, follow the action steps below which work best for you. These proactive precautions can be your personal recipes for survival and sobriety at holiday time. Happy holidays!

Action Plan

- Don't expect too much. Holidays seldom live up to expectations.
- Talk over your fears with your sponsor and/or a supportive family member in advance.
- Practice "turn down" phrases (Appendix B).
- Use proven strategies for coping with holidays overall (See Trap #23).
- Boost your confidence with positive self affirmations (See Appendix D).
- Show up late . . . Leave early.
- Hold on to your AA medallion. (It's a tangible reminder of whom you are and how far you've come.)
- Talk about your sobriety. (If you're comfortable, it usually helps to get feelings out on the table.)
- Take a walk after dinner.
- Associate with the right family members (the sober

ones).

- Concentrate on others. Lose yourself. Be attentive. Spend time really listening.
- Look for the humor in the situation. It's there.

Trap #3 - Family Reunions

If family is part of your drinking problem, any gathering of the extended clan is like a reunion from hell. A reunion often takes all the most unpleasant and uncomfortable elements of ordinary family holidays and celebrations and multiplies them by the number of relatives in attendance. This is classic relapse material.

When you're new to the world of sobriety, a family reunion may be an unfair test. It can feel like a gathering of all your worst critics in one place at one time for the sole purpose of humiliating you. Of course, the truth is that most people at the reunion won't spend much time talking about you or even noticing you. You and your new sobriety aren't as important to others as they are to you.

Family reunions are noisy, hectic and tiring at best. At worst, they can be nasty and depressing. The good thing is, they don't last very long and they don't happen very often. When you're ready, you'll find you can handle family reunions even better now that you're sober. You may even learn to enjoy them!

Of course, like other family gatherings, celebrations and holidays, a reunion may be too much to take during early recovery. If so, "pass" and don't feel guilty.

Realize though, you can't run or hide forever. When you're prepared, the strategies below can get you through any reunion with your sanity, sobriety and self esteem intact.

The tougher the test, the better it feels when you pass it. Recovery is made up of passing lots of little tests and a few big ones. A family reunion is a big one. Go for it!

Action Plan

▸ Write down all of the strengths and qualities you appreciate about your family. Look over the list several times before going to the reunion. (It speeds healing and forgiveness.)

▸ Talk about the upcoming reunion with your AA group or sponsor.

▸ Practice your conversations in advance.

▸ Go to the reunion with your eyes open. Realize that all families have problems.

▸ Recite the Serenity Prayer before, during and after the reunion. Think about it. What the prayer says applies particularly to family relationships.

▸ Follow the action steps for Trap #31 (Class Reunions).

▸ Believe you have changed.

▸ Attend with a nondrinker. Agree to leave together as soon as you feel too much pressure.

▸ Be honest about your drinking, your sobriety and your recovery.

▸ Don't pretend or act like you're drinking. You won't fool anyone–not even yourself.

▸ Spend time with the children at the reunion. (They're

the nonjudgmental members of the family.)
- ► Monitor your feelings and work off any mounting tension by breathing deeply or walking around. Don't let anger, resentment or frustration build up.
- ► Eat a lot--but nothing salty.
- ► Reward yourself big time when the reunion is over and you've successfully passed up a prime opportunity to relapse. (See Appendix E.)

Trap #4 - Parenting Tensions

As a recovering alcoholic, just taking care of yourself feels like a full-time job. Taking care of a family often seems overwhelming. Can you stay sober, build a new life and be an effective parent at the same time? You bet you can! Still, it won't be easy. Being a parent never is.

Parenting tensions can test sobriety. Relapse is always an option. However, parenting can also become the anchor of your recovery. It all depends on the choices you make.

Parenting isn't for wimps (neither is recovery.) It's a 24-hour a day job with few vacations and no retirement. When the pressures and problems of parenting begin to mount up, recovering alcoholics run the risk of relapse. It doesn't go away.

Raising children means facing a long series of relapse traps but falling off the wagon is never an acceptable parenting technique. As a parent, you may have lots of reasons to start drinking again. Your children are your best reasons not to.

Although parenting is never completely relapse-proof, help is available. Use the action plans below to become the kind of parent your child deserves and to stay clean and sober in the process. It doesn't get any better than that!

Action Plan

- Educate your family about relapse traps and the warning signs of a pending slip. Give them permission to be the watchdogs over your recovery.
- Don't stop going to meetings just because you're a busy parent; take your family along sometimes.
- Involve family members in Alanon when appropriate.
- Join M.A.D.D. (Mothers Against Drunk Driving). Better yet, get actively involved.
- Try to get a sponsor who is also a parent.
- Start a Not-To-Do List containing all the activities and behaviors you know you need to avoid to stay sober.
- Read the Big Book of Alcoholics Anonymous every day.
- Don't keep alcohol in the house.
- Find ways to have family fun without drinking. (See Appendix C).
- Don't even try to be the perfect parent. You'll be setting yourself up for failure and increasing the likelihood of relapse.
- Whenever you're tempted to drink, try to think of the last time alcohol helped you solve any problem.
- Teach your children about your disease. You'll re-learn some important lessons in the process.
- Remember the bad times in the good times. It will help keep you from getting overly-complacent.

- No matter how busy your family activities, save time for yourself.
- Involve the whole family in celebrating your sobriety anniversary (birthday).
- Stick to a budget. Money problems undermine both your family and your sobriety.
- Make communication the #1 priority in your family.
- Simplify your family life (K.I.S.S.). Why not buy a canoe instead of a high-tech speed boat?
- Read *Mothers' Wisdom* and *501 Ways to Boost Your Child's Self Esteem* (Contemporary Books) for more tips on making parenting manageable–and fun.
- If family problems or pressures begin to build up, join a parent support group or get family counseling BEFORE things get out of hand.
- Work on the spiritual side of your marriage and your sobriety. You don't get better at praying without practice.

Trap #5 - Divorce

"Drinking causes divorce. Divorce causes drinking. It's a vicious cycle."   Anon.

Going through a divorce is painful for anyone. For a drunk trying to hang onto sobriety and put together a new beginning, it can be devastating. Of all the family-related relapse traps, divorce is the most dangerous.

Divorce pulls the rug out from almost everything you call normal. It wipes out a major anchor of your life; it shatters your self esteem; it calls into question your basic self worth; it makes you feel vulnerable and alone; it turns your economic life upside down; it hurts and it's scary. Divorce sets into motion all the conditions which facilitate relapse. However, relapse doesn't have to happen.

The same skills, tools and support that have helped you through recovery this far can help you get through divorce without slipping. As painful as divorce is, it positions you for fresh opportunities. Divorce is the end of a marriage and a relationship. That's all. You can make it the beginning of something better–including a stronger recovery and a better life.

Self-pity won't keep you sober during divorce. Taking positive action will. The steps below show you how. Just do it!

Action Plan

- Renew your emphasis on taking life "one day at a time." It's the only way to recover from divorce.
- If children are involved, focus more on their needs and less on your own.
- Talk to friends (sober friends) who have gone through divorce. How did they survive?
- Let your lawyer handle unpleasant negotiations. Save your strength for moving on.
- Attend as many AA meetings as it takes to keep you on track. (Two or three meetings a day is not too many.)
- Keep working the 12 steps. This may be the time to take on more 12th step work (carrying the message to others).
- Don't waste time trying to fix blame. Blaming

requires looking backward. You need to move forward.

- Check the Action Plan for Trap #25 (Break-Ups).
- Keep busy. Take on new responsibilities at work. Revitalize old hobbies. Take a class. Do whatever it takes to stay active and involved in life.
- Don't look for other chemical answers to your problems. Be careful about taking tranquilizers or sleeping pills. You can't medicate the pain of divorce away.
- Pray and attend church–a lot.
- Have long talks with your sponsor. Freely vent your feelings, anger and resentments. That's what sponsors are for.
- Become physical. Exercise, jog, learn karate or join a bowling league. (Most cities have at least one "dry" bowling alley.)
- Write in a journal all the problems divorce will eliminate from your life. Reread the entries often so you stay focused on the future. Things will get better–without alcohol.
- Don't rush into a ricochet romance. Take time to get your act together.
- Go back into After Care Treatment for a while if necessary.
- Take personal inventory. (This may be a good time to do another Step 4.) Concentrate on all the things you still have for which you can be grateful.
- Use self affirmations to boost your confidence. (See Appendix D.)
- Join a support group for recently divorced people.
- Go back to basics. Grow close to nature again.

(Nature has a healing effect.)
- ▸ Let go of the past. Let your Higher Power take care of the future.

Trap #6 - Death of a Family Member

The death of a loved one or family member is always painful. It rips a hole in our lives and reminds us of our own mortality. Worse yet, it triggers a whole series of unwelcome feelings. (We should have done more, said more and been there more.) These are especially difficult feelings for recovering alcoholics to deal with. That's why Guilt and Grief are often the honor guards of Relapse.

The great benefit of being clean and sober at a time of family sorrow or crisis is that you know clearly what's going on, you can actually help and you are fully aware of your own true feelings and emotions. Don't screw it up by getting drunk.

Relapse will only add to your loss. Better ways to handle grief and guilt are available. The following steps won't make the pain go away but they can keep you from losing your sobriety in addition to your family member.

Action Plan

- ▸ Stay away from wakes if you are not sure you can handle them.
- ▸ Attend an AA meeting as soon as possible before and after the viewing and the funeral.

- Help in any way you can. Help with funeral arrangements, be a pall bearer, record cards, flowers and memorials. When you are busy helping, you're not thinking about drinking.
- Distance yourself from family members who think drinking is a natural part of the grief process.
- Talk about your pain and loss with your AA group and your sponsor.
- Give yourself permission to grieve. Let the full grieving process play out. Don't try to rush it or to skip any of the steps. Allow yourself to experience all the natural feelings of disbelief, denial, anger and acceptance.
- Don't just be sad. Find a way to "celebrate" the life of the deceased (with other family members if possible).
- Talk to the deceased if it helps. Lots of people talk to dead friends and loved ones. (George Burns held grave side chats with Gracie for years.)
- Cherish the lessons you learned from the deceased. Write them in your journal for future reference and reflection.
- Practice prayer and meditation. You'll never need them more.
- Use journal or poetry writing to let out your emotions.
- Try some of the steps in the Action Plan for Trap #34 (Loss of a Friend).
- Recite the Serenity Prayer and allow it to work for you.
- Watch out for signs of depression. If feelings of sorrow and hopelessness persist over a long period, seek medical help.

- Consider taking a grief education class, joining an adult grief support group or seeking grief counseling. Many health care providers offer all of these services.
- Look for other ways to atone if you haven't made amends with the deceased. Can you do something for other surviving family members? Can you help the deceased's favorite charity or cause?
- Make a vow to the deceased that you will continue your sobriety in honor of his or her memory. (This is one vow you won't want to break.)
- Look to the children in the family for proof that life goes on. They symbolize hope and continuity.
- Forgive the deceased–and forgive yourself.

SECTION II

TRAPS AT
WORK

Section II

TRAPS AT WORK

For many of us, work is central to our lives. It not only supports us; it defines us. Your job isn't just what you do; it's who you are. That's why drunks (practicing and recovering) struggle to keep their job separate from their disease.

Work is so precious that it's often the last place you allow any signs of progressive alcoholism to show up. (Your family may be falling apart but if things are okay at work, maybe you'll make it after all.) You lie, hide, cheat–anything to keep your job. While you show up for work most days and do your job marginally well, you can't be too lost, can you? However, if you lose your job because of drinking, it's almost as if you've lost your very soul to the disease you try so hard to deny.

Continuing to work is important to every desperate drunk. Returning to work is equally crucial to most recovering alcoholics. Unfortunately, the workplace is full of relapse traps. Most jobs involve some pressures, problems, risks, temptations, frustrations, highs, lows, competition, conflict, stress, disappointments, unfairness, wins, losses and too many bosses. All friends of relapse!

At work, you can find many chances and reasons to relapse. Opportunities for success on the job every day are also there. Look for them. Lasting recovery is built one small success at a time.

Staying sober at work can be hard work. Section II

will make it easier. It pinpoints the most common workplace reasons for relapse and provides the tools necessary to skirt them. It's up to you to use these tools. Many successful people in every field and profession are recovering drunks. You can be one of them too. If you can get high on work, who needs booze?

Trap #7 - Returning to Work After Treatment

Returning to work after hitting bottom, drying out or going through treatment is a trial by ordeal for most recovering alcoholics. The stakes are high and so are the risks.

Facing friends and co-workers who know about your problem-drinking raises serious issues of guilt, shame and embarrassment. Self doubt is inevitable. Will they accept you? Can you regain trust? Will everyone be talking about you behind your back? Can you still do the job? Will it ever be like it was? Can you make it?

The answer is, "Of course you can." Your co-workers won't be nearly as worried about it as you are. If you do the job, they will accept you. You may be amazed at how forgiving people are–and how forgetful. You'll probably find more support than you may deserve. Eventually, you may earn greater respect than ever because you're overcoming an illness which kills so many. Likewise, recovery can make you a better, happier and more productive worker. It happens every day. It can happen to you.

Going back to work is never easy but it is necessary. The workplace is often the best and only place to fully reclaim your dignity and self esteem. Of course, in a few instances, you may find an employer who is behind the times, fellow workers who are insensitive and a work environment which is hostile. If this happens, it's the wrong job anyway. Get another job.

Most of the time, returning to the job will be easier than you would ever imagine. Don't build up false fears. Don't underestimate the capacity of others to care. After all, recovery requires a little faith.

Success in avoiding relapse is like any other success on the job. You must plan your work and work your plan. Here are some simple steps to help you win back your niche in the workplace and stay alcohol-free in the process.

Action Plan

- Concentrate on doing the job. Concentrate on your work. Don't think about what you're missing by not drinking or worry about what others think.
- Expect some awkward moments and some skepticism about your sobriety. If this reaction comes as no surprise, it's less likely to trigger a relapse.
- Accept support from others. It's okay to allow people to care and help.
- Don't expect any special treatment. If you do, you'll be disappointed.
- Change your routines. Don't pick up where you left off (i.e., having lunch at your favorite watering hole or stopping by a popular gathering place with old drinking buddies after work). A new beginning calls for new routines.

- Seek out extra support (AA meetings, recovering friends, sponsor, etc.) during the first few weeks back on the job.
- Practice much positive self talk during the early stages of returning to work. (See Appendix D.)
- Go to the gym instead of a bar at the times you used to drink (i.e., lunchtime, right after work, etc.).
- Be careful about joining co-workers for Happy Hour on Fridays (T.G.I.F.). If you go, have some "Turn Down" phrases ready to use. (See Appendix B.)
- Make amends to the people at work whom you harmed, cheated or disappointed while you were drinking.
- Accept that you may be watched closer than usual. It's more pressure, but it's also an opportunity to model sobriety for others who may have drinking problems.
- Associate with non-drinking co-workers.
- Remember your priorities--God, family, work, sobriety. Drinking doesn't make the list.
- Ask for feedback. You know you're feeling better and working better. It helps to hear it from others.
- Maintain balance in your life. Keep your job in perspective. You work to live. You don't live to work.
- Enjoy your job but don't go overboard. Becoming a workaholic isn't recovery. It's substituting one addictive behavior for another.
- Keep your boss and supervisor informed of your progress. Show them the medallions you receive on your sobriety anniversary dates. Pride feels better when it's shared.

- Don't play Carrie Nation. It's not your job to save all the drunks you work with. If you try, the backlash may drive you to drink yourself.
- Reward yourself for every day you work and don't drink. (See Appendix E.)

Trap #8 - Good News At Work (New Job, Promotion, Raise, Bonus, etc.)

Good things happen to good people. Unfortunately for recovering alcoholics, bad news sometimes follows good.

A new job, a promotion, a raise or a bonus is quite heady stuff. Flushed with good fortune, it's easy to feel back in control again. Alcohol isn't the only thing that produces euphoria or self delusion.

Feeling vulnerable can contribute to a slip; but feeling invincible is even more dangerous. Humility promotes recovery; cockiness favors relapse.

Drunks aren't always good at accepting compliments, good news, prosperity or success. We're easily blinded. It's hard for alcoholics–even recovering ones–to stay grounded.

The advice below can help keep you on track when good news strikes. Use these tips to accept success or good fortune, to enjoy it, to recognize it for what it really is and to use it to reinforce your recovery.

No matter how many good things happen to you at work, the best news continues to be your sobriety. It can last a lot longer than any transitory good fortune. Don't let good news at work derail your recovery.

Action Plan

▸ Include your family in any celebration with co-workers. The presence of family members will help keep you humble (and sober).

▸ Shy away from celebrations where they serve booze. As a recovering alcoholic, you don't need people toasting you or offering to buy you drinks.

▸ Share the good news with AA friends. You can celebrate safely with them.

▸ Give credit to others. Diverting attention from yourself helps diffuse pressures which can lead to relapse.

▸ Remember what contributed to your "good news." Hint: It wasn't alcohol.

▸ Keep on doing what's worked for you thus far–including staying sober.

▸ Revisit Steps I and II. When things are going well, it's easy to forget "powerless over alcohol" or the need to "turn things over to God as we understood Him."

▸ Remember that alcohol is "cunning, baffling and powerful." Don't allow yourself to become overconfident. You'll only be setting yourself up for a fall.

▸ You deserve to have good things happen, but give your Higher Power some credit too.

▸ Watch out for the warning signs of a relapse in the making. (Appendix A) If you see one coming, call your sponsor immediately. It's never too early to get help.

- Keep your AA medallion handy. Hold on to it to keep in touch with reality.
- Don't fall into the Attitude Traps of "False Pride" or "Complacency." Follow the action plans outlined in Section VI instead.
- Concentrate on your next goal. Enjoy the moment and move on. Don't get stuck in your work or your recovery.

Trap #9 - Bad News At Work (Blown Deal, Passed Over, Laid Off, Downsized, etc.)

"Things go bad. They get better. Every job has its little problems. That's why they call them 'jobs', not 'summer camp.'"   Harvey MacKay

Inevitably, something bad happens in every job. Your best deal may blow up. They may pass you over for a promotion or new job. They may even lay you off. No work is problem-free.

Most people can accept negative episodes or setbacks at work as part of normal living. They handle them and move on. It's not always that easy for recovering alcoholics. What seems like a bump along the way for many, can be the end of the road for someone trying to stay sober.

It doesn't take much bad news to knock the props from under a freshly constructed recovery. Most drunks, new to sobriety, usually feel very vulnerable, unsure and afraid. Their insecurity often magnifies work-related problems. When you're used to scurrying for a bottle at the first sign of trouble, you don't have many problem-solving skills to fall back on. Even minor setbacks can be all it takes to push a fledgling recoveree over the edge into relapse.

Fortunately, there are proven ways for recovering alcoholics to cope with problems that arise in the workplace. Select from the suggestions below to design your personal workplace survival plan. The good news about bad news at work is that every problem situation you survive or overcome on the job makes you stronger. Do it for yourself!

Action Plan

▸ Try' to find out why things went wrong. If it's correctable, do something about it. If not, let it go. (Sound familiar? It's the Serenity Prayer in action.)

▸ If you actually lose your job, take action immediately. The worst thing you can do is sit around brooding. Start looking. Use your network of AA contacts. (It's better than an employment agency.) Don't forget to sign up for unemployment compensation if you qualify.

▸ Use the RADAR problem-solving method recommended by AA . . .

Recognize the real problem.
Accept the problem as your own.
Detach yourself to gain objectivity.
Accept help.
Respond with action.

▸ Stick to familiar rituals. You may need structure to remind yourself that everything isn't falling apart.

- Seek a safe environment where you don't feel rejected. Do something with your family. Go to church. Attend lots of AA meetings.
- Don't fall prey to the Attitude Traps of "Why me?" or "I don't care." Use applicable action steps from Section VI.
- Load up with self affirmations. (See Appendix D.)
- List what's still going right in your life.
- Pray. Do your best and then turn responsibility for outcomes over to your Higher Power.
- Listen to recovery tapes for inspiration. (You can even listen while driving to job interviews.)
- Create something beautiful or useful. Do something you're proud of. It will draw your attention from the "bad news" at work and re-validate your worth.
- Get mad. Get even. Just don't get drunk.
- Increase your level of preparation. Respond to setbacks with renewed effort.
- Reevaluate your priorities. Sobriety should still come out on top.
- When things get really bad, pamper yourself even more. (See Appendix E.)

Trap #10 - Performance Reviews

We all need feedback to grow. One anonymous commentator explains, "The truth will set you free, but first it will p--- you off." As long as you work, you will be evaluated periodically. Get used to it–you don't have to like it.

Most people get apprehensive at evaluation time. It's

the most intense pressure point of the work year. Job evaluations need to be taken seriously. It's okay to be concerned about them, but they aren't worth relapsing over.

Performance reviews are like report cards for adults. No one wants a failing grade. The results can effect future employment status, levels of compensation, bonus amounts and chances for promotion. It's no wonder lots of workers would like a stiff drink to build confidence before going into a performance review situation and another one to help them celebrate or forget afterwards. (Don't even think about it!)

As a drunk-gone-dry, a performance review can be a pivotal point in your recovery. Sometimes, it doesn't take much negative criticism to crack your veneer of self confidence. A positive review can be a milestone in your sobriety. A negative one, however, can reinforce preexisting feelings of low self esteem and worthlessness. Relapses are made of things like this.

The best advice for recovering alcoholics is to accept performance reviews as a natural process in the workplace. Recognize them for what they are. An evaluation is a snapshot of how things look at the moment. They're not an obituary summing up your entire life's work. Performance reviews can get better (or worse) over time. It's up to you. If your review is positive, it boosts your recovery. Accept it and use it to do even better. If it's negative, here are some ways to handle it without alcohol.

Action Plan

- Don't worry too much in advance. Anxiety won't change the evaluation. Besides, your worst worries rarely materialize.
- Listen carefully during the evaluation conference. Be sure you hear exactly what was said. Ask for clarification if necessary.
- Request specific suggestions on how you can correct deficiencies. Follow-up on any recommendations you receive.
- Don't overreact. Don't react at all immediately. Take time to internalize what it all means.
- Put things in perspective. Remind yourself that no one is perfect. (Even Babe Ruth struck our 1333 times.) As Zig Ziglar says, "Failure is an event, not a person."
- Use self affirmations to counteract negative criticism. (See Appendix D.)
- Share the evaluation results with people who care about and support you–family, sober friends, AA group, sponsor, mentors, etc. These people are your safety nets.
- Ask yourself, "Was it fair?" Take your own inventory. You know better than anyone how you're doing.
- Remind yourself that drinking won't change or make this evaluation any better. It can, however, make the next one worse.
- Don't make excuses. Learn from the evaluation. Act on it. Make an improvement plan. Request the resources you need to acquire new skills and get better at your job.

- If the evaluation is inaccurate or unfair, speak up. Be assertive. File an appeal. Write a rebuttal to include in your personnel record.
- Remember, no matter what mistakes you've made on the job, if you're still sober you're doing something right!

Trap #11 - Customer/Client Pressures

The customer isn't always right. In fact, some customers or clients are all wrong for recovering alcoholics.

We all know a few hard-drinking customers who like to mix booze and business and consummate deals over cocktails. Often, these clients expect (or demand) the people with whom they do business to drink with them as well.

It's hard to turn down a drink from a good customer with money to spend. We've all been trained to please customers, not go against their wishes. Sometimes, you have to forget your training. This is one of those times.

As tempting as it may be, don't succumb to customer or client pressures to use alcohol. Never be fooled into thinking that "just one little drink won't make any difference." It will. If you cheat on your recovery once, it will be much easier to slip a second time and a third–that's called relapse.

When the price of doing business is drinking, do business elsewhere. Even if you blow a deal or lose a customer, it's always good business to put your sobriety first.

Initially, recovery is often a little wobbly. Pressures from customers or clients can topple it if you let them. Don't let them. Instead, implement the action plan for handling customer/client pressures outlined below. You'll be glad you did.

Action Plan

- Try to find an AA group with members who have similar jobs or business interests. Ask them how they handle "difficult" customers.
- Arrange breakfast meetings instead of business luncheons with customers who drink.
- If you have to "do lunch" with these customers, make reservations at an alcohol-free restaurant.
- When you must have lunch with the customer where they serve alcohol, at least stay away from the smoking section.
- If you're comfortable with it, be up front. Tell the customer you're in recovery. Your client or customer may respect you more for your honesty.
- Don't try to change your customer's drinking habits. Avoid preaching about alcohol or you'll chase away your client's business for sure. Remember AA's public relations policy, "attraction, not promotion."
- Practice turn-down phrases ahead of time until you're comfortable using them. (See Appendix B.)
- Never agree to do business during Happy Hour unless you're rock solid in your recovery. Even then, take along a sober associate.
- Let someone else take over the customer or the account. You may lose a little business but you'll

gain ground in your recovery. That makes you the winner.

Trap #12 - A Boozing Boss

If your boss is a heavy drinker, your recovery may be in double jeopardy. Not only may you be denied much-needed support, but your boss may even punish you for trying to stay clean and sober. It's common for a boozing boss to feel resentful of an employee who is recovering.

If your sobriety threatens your boss's denial, you may be ignored, treated unfairly, subjected to "dirty tricks" or, even sabotaged in your job. Working under these conditions is a severe test for any recovering alcoholic. People have relapsed for a lot less.

Maybe a drunk trying to stay sober shouldn't work for a drunk who's still drinking. The sensible thing may be to seek employment in a more supportive environment. You'll have to decide.

If you are determined to stick it out and try to make it work, these strategies will help. Good luck!

Action Plan

- ► Focus on your work. Keep a low profile and reduce direct contact with the boss. Use an associate or secretary as a buffer.
- ► Seek out other sober employees. How do they get along with the boss?
- ► Since you won't be getting much support from your supervisor at work, beef up your external support

34

system. Go to more AA meetings. Have daily contact with your sponsor. Read as much uplifting literature as possible.

- Pray a lot. It will take some help from your Higher Power to get you past this relapse trap.
- Show that you mean business about your recovery. Don't waver, don't waffle and don't give in to temptation, pressure or coercion. When your boss sees you're serious about sobriety, he or she may leave you alone. Maybe, your boss will eventually even ask how it works.
- Let your family know what you're going through. Their support is crucial.
- Work one day at a time.
- Unless asked, don't talk about your recovery in front of your boss. It may seem like you're flaunting your sobriety.
- Don't talk to your boss about his or her drinking. You may trigger more resentment and retaliation. Concentrate on your own sobriety. That's about all you can handle at first.
- Observe what drinking is doing to your boss. It can help reinforce your own recovery.
- Begin to develop Plan B. Start looking for other options. Build a network of contacts in case things don't work out. Having a back up plan will bolster your confidence and performance.
- Consider seeking a transfer to a more favorable environment.
- If you suffer abuse or unfair treatment, document the incidents and complain to the Personnel Department or your union representative. Don't be bullied out of

your job or your sobriety.
- Confront your boss about perceived ill-treatment or injustices if necessary. It's risky, but it may clear the air. Be sure to have a witness.
- Reward yourself frequently for successfully "hanging in there." (See Appendix E.)

Trap #13 - Business Luncheons

Business luncheons are a popular way to strike deals while combining socializing and work. It's a civilized way of doing business. It can also be a sneaky way to mix booze and business.

Sometimes, business luncheons are just another excuse to drink. They rank among the most dangerous work-related relapse traps. Peer pressure and false pride can make it hard to say "No" to a few drinks as part of clinching a profitable deal. Look out! The 3-martini lunch has cut short countless recoveries. It can threaten yours as well.

As drinking habits and rules for deducting business expenses change, the popularity of business luncheons and the pressures to do business over cocktails is lessening–but they haven't gone away. It still pays for recovering alcoholics to keep their guard up whenever business and alcohol go together. Don't let a working luncheon turn into a drinking lunch–it's a risk not worth taking.

It's natural to be uncomfortable about handling business luncheons during recovery but don't let that stop you. Instead, let the measures below help you "do lunch" and do business without sacrificing your sobriety. It's easier than you think!

Action Plan

- ► Whenever possible, substitute breakfast meetings for business luncheons.
- ► Try to arrange all your business luncheons at alcohol-free restaurants.
- ► Show up early and have your coffee or soda served before the drinking crowd arrives.
- ► Arrive a little late–after cocktail orders have been taken.
- ► Have some ready-made refusal phrases in mind. (See Appendix B.)
- ► Take along a non-drinking colleague for support.
- ► Turn your wine glass over immediately. It provides a cue for the table server.
- ► Order your food as soon as possible.
- ► Take care of business first if you can. Then, if drinking gets serious, you can excuse yourself.
- ► If you really feel out of place drinking soda, order non-alcoholic beer. Most people won't notice the difference.
- ► If the atmosphere and ambiance of the occasion triggers a craving, know it will pass shortly. Wait it out.
- ► Reward yourself when it's over. (See Appendix E.)

Trap #14 - T.G.I.F.

Friday is the hardest day of the week to stay sober. In our society, Fridays are designated drinking days. Celebrating the end of the work week at Happy Hour is a tradition. It starts in college and it doesn't end until retirement.

T.G.I.F. is a rallying cry for everyone to gather after work on Fridays for the sole purpose of drinking and/or getting drunk. Recovering alcoholics couldn't find a worse situation.

Friday is prime time for a slip. Fridays are going to be a big test of your sobriety if T.G.I.F. was a big thing in your drinking life. Keep in mind–tests are made for passing.

You can survive T.G.I.F. and stay sober. The action plan below will serve as a survival guide. You can even learn to celebrate the end of the work week without alcohol and actually enjoy it. It takes preparation, planning and discipline but it's definitely worth it. If you can stay sober Friday, the rest of the week is a piece of cake.

Action Plan

▸ During the early stages of recovery, if you're afraid you might cave-in to T.G.I.F. temptations or pressures take Friday afternoons off or leave work early on Fridays.

▸ Not everybody at work drinks. Find out what the nondrinkers do Friday after work.

▸ Make Friday FAMILY NIGHT. Plan special alcohol-free activities the whole family will enjoy. (See Appendix C.) It's not a substitute for Happy Hour–it's better!

- Find a Friday evening AA meeting to attend. (Many cities have special Open Speaker Meetings on Fridays.)
- Follow some of the stay-sober suggestions for Trap #22-Party Time
- Plan your personal T.G.I.F. celebration. Do something you really like to do after work on Friday (i.e., browse in a bookstore or music store, get a massage, etc.).
- Later, if you decide to go with the gang on Friday, brush up on your turn-down phrases ahead of time. (See Appendix B.)
- Always carry a list of negative consequences you've suffered because of drinking. Review it before showing up for Happy Hour.
- Limit your exposure. The first time back at Happy Hour, just make an appearance. Leave early.
- Stick with water, soft drinks or juice. If you get a craving for a "real drink," postpone taking the first one until the craving passes.
- Concentrate on the food at Happy Hour. It's often free. If you fill up on food, you won't have room for booze. (Reminder: Stay away from salty items.)
- Carry your sobriety anniversary medallion as a reminder of where you've been, where you are and where you want to stay.
- Watch how other people behave at Happy Hour. It's a powerful argument for sobriety. T.G.I.F. = Thank God, I'm Free!

Trap #15 - Company Athletic Teams (The Softball Syndrome)

Many businesses sponsor employee sports teams (i.e., softball, bowling, etc.) to boost morale and promote public relations. It's good fun and good exercise. It's also another great opportunity to drink.

What's better than a cold beer after a summer softball game? How about a cold six-pack or case or keg? Sometimes, the post-game party becomes more important than the game itself.

To make matters worse, local bars often offer two-for-one drink specials to company sports teams. It's no wonder that lots of employees come for the sport, stay for the party and end up getting drunk. Don't be one of them.

If you're like most alcoholics, you want to please, get along, fit in. It is hard not to want to be a part of the group and that makes it difficult to avoid drinking with the crowd after a hard-fought game. The thrill of victory and the agony of defeat makes players thirsty. The emotions and excitement of sports make it difficult to remain objective so sports teams may not be the best activity for recovering alcoholics. It's not worth it, if relapse becomes part of the post-game show.

Don't sign up for a company team if you're uncertain about resisting the temptations and pressures of post-game parties. Winning a game is useless if you're going to strike out afterwards. Wait until your confidence and your sobriety are more firmly entrenched. When you do decide to join the team, here are some rules to play by.

Action Plan

- Tell your teammates upfront about your sobriety status. Most likely, they will respect it and, then forget it.
- Make an appointment or commitment for immediately after the game. This will give you an excuse to "pass" on the post-game party.
- Invite family members to be spectators. They can help you make a graceful exit before the post-game drinking begins in earnest.
- Have an excuse for skipping the post-game party (i.e., "I have to go to work early tomorrow." "I have lots of paperwork to do tonight." Etc.).
- Find a reason to leave before the game is over.
- Find an AA meeting to go to after the game.
- Rehearse some refusal phrases until you're comfortable with them. (See Appendix B.)
- Bring your own soft drinks for the post-game party.
- Offer to pour or serve drinks–just don't drink any. Keeping busy is a stay-sober survival technique.
- Volunteer to be the designated driver.
- If the team goes to a bar to party, alert the bartender that you're not drinking alcohol.
- Find something other than alcohol to use for celebrating victory or sloughing off defeat. How about pizza or ice cream–or both?

Trap #16 - Office Parties

Although they are getting better, office parties are notorious for encouraging heavy drinking. In some corporate cultures, the whole purpose of these parties is for everyone to get smashed–with permission. Obviously, these events create a hostile environment for anyone trying to stay sober.

Unfortunately, office parties are often command performances. Everyone is expected to attend. Once there, everyone is expected to drink. The booze is free and there's plenty of it.

This can be pretty intimidating if you're a recovering alcoholic. You don't know how to act. You're already walking on eggs. You don't want to offend anyone. You don't want to be a wet blanket, but you also don't want to take that first drink. The good news is you don't have to.

Anyone just out of treatment or unsure of their sobriety doesn't need the pressures of a high octane office party. Many ugly things can happen at these parties–including the first slip toward relapse. It's safer to stay away from them at first.

However, you'll need a plan if you have to go. Use the steps below to make a plan fitting your circumstances. They really do work.

After the initial jitters, you may find that you actually have more fun at an office party without drinking–and you'll feel a whole lot better in the morning. Enjoy!

Action Plan

- Lobby for alcohol-free office parties. You may be surprised by how much support you get.
- Volunteer to serve on the planning committee. That will give you a chance to include plenty of non-alcoholic beverages on the menu.
- Don't go. Explain to your boss in advance why the party isn't a safe place for you to be at this point in your recovery.
- If you're really worried about the party, call in sick the day of the party.
- If you go, call your sponsor for a last minute pep-talk just before you leave.
- Don't stay long. Swoop in. Be seen. Swoop out.
- Spend time at the party with other employees who are nondrinkers. There's a lot more of them than you ever noticed when you were drinking.
- Allow yourself to feel smug in the knowledge you're going to remember what happened at the party.
- If all they serve is alcoholic beverages, drink water.
- Keep moving. Keep talking. Be ready to leave if the pressure gets to be too much.
- For more coping strategies, see Trap #22 (Party Time).

Trap #17 - Overnight Business Travel

It's hard enough to stay sober in a familiar environment surrounded by family, friends and supporters. It's a lot harder if you're alone in a strange place. That's why overnight business travel isn't always a good idea during the early phases of recovery.

Business trips can be risky business when you're just beginning your sobriety. You have too much free time; too much time alone; too much temptation; too much anonymity; too much adrenaline; and too much opportunity–including an expense account and an honor bar in your hotel room.

Sobriety thrives on structure. Taking away familiar routines can be a sure way to give alcohol a second chance. Overnight business travel is a potentially lethal relapse trap–and you're the prey. Travel is fun. Relapse isn't. Always be extra careful when you're on the road.

Try to put off travel for the first few weeks after getting sober. If you have to travel on your job, let AA, not AAA, be your travel guide. You can have a safe and sober trip the first time and every time if you follow the simple precautions below.

Action Plan

▸ If you fly, go coach where the drinks aren't free.
▸ Cut short your trip. Don't stay overnight if you can help it.

- Try to plan your trip to avoid staying over the weekend. Saturday night in a strange city feels especially lonely. Loneliness is often a forerunner of relapse.
- Take along a family member or sober companion for support if possible.
- Call your family and your sponsor every day.
- Bring along plenty of inspirational literature to read.
- Always carry your sobriety anniversary medallion. It's a little piece of conscience in your pocket. Don't leave home without it.
- Focus on the work. Put in long hours. Work hard. Then, get plenty of rest.
- Don't hang out in the bars. Go where the sober people go.
- Don't even think about picking up a date on an overnight business trip. It almost always involves alcohol. Besides, illicit romance and relapse frequently go together.
- Work out in the hotel spa.
- Eat at coffee shops and health food or fast food restaurants that don't serve liquor.
- Visit a local AA meeting. You're always welcome–it may be the highlight of your trip.
- Keep busy. Go window shopping. Take in a movie. Visit the library. Go to church. Walk in a local park. Just don't spend too much time alone in your room.
- If you get really edgy or depressed, call the local AA. They can put you into contact with a temporary, on-site sponsor.

Trap #18 - Foreign Assignments

Try moving to another country if you think overnight business travel is hard on sobriety. An assignment to work in a foreign country can be a dream come true for some people. For others, it can be a nightmare. For a recovering alcoholic, it all depends on where you're assigned.

Your abstinence may be easier if you're sent to a third world, Islamic nation that prohibits the use of alcohol. On the other hand, if you're assigned to a country like Japan, where drinking is the norm and where booze and business is interwoven, your recovery may be in serious trouble. Wherever you go, you won't be alone. AA is everywhere.

It's probably better not to be separated from loved ones and supporters early in recovery. However, if you have no choice, here's some advice you can count on to help you stay clean and sober while working in a foreign land. Bon voyage!

Action Plan

- Take AA with you. Pack the Big Book. Read it daily.
- Keep working the 12 steps. They're just as helpful in Tokyo as they are in Toledo.
- Don't let distance make you become remote from your program of sobriety. Use the telephone and the internet (e-mail) to stay in touch with your home AA group and your sponsor.

- Use the worldwide network of AA to find a group near where you will be living. If there isn't any, consider starting one. Doing Twelfth Step work for others is a good way to stay sober yourself.
- If you're comfortable, be upfront with your foreign hosts and business associates. Tell them about your sobriety status. They'll probably understand. After all, alcoholism is a worldwide problem.
- Devote yourself to learning as much as possible about the culture of your adopted land. The busier you are, the better. Recovering drunks don't need a whole lot of idle time on their hands.
- Use prayer and meditation to keep on track. These are tools that work anywhere.
- Surround yourself with recovery reminders. Stick post-it notes inscribed with AA slogans throughout your living quarters.
- Make new friends–sober friends–as soon as possible.
- Work on your spiritual life. Reconnect with your church. Attending services in another country can give you a new perspective and strengthen your faith. You need faith to stay sober when you're far from home.
- Understand the difference between being alone and being lonely. (As a foreigner, you may be alone a lot.) Learn to enjoy your own company.
- Maintain a regular schedule of waking and sleeping. You're more likely to relapse if your system gets off balance.

- Keep a journal. It's a better outlet than guzzling booze.
- Monitor your emotions. If you feel yourself beginning to slip and don't seem able to stop it, ask to be sent home AS SOON AS POSSIBLE!

Trap #19 - Vacations

There's a reason so many top executives refuse to take vacations. It's called fear. They're afraid they can't handle the pressure of no pressure. They're frightened by idleness. Days without deadlines scare the hell out of them. The same is true for many recovering alcoholics.

The worst of all the relapse traps associated with work can be not working. For many alcoholics, vacation is the hardest time of all to stay sober. You're probably more likely to relapse while on vacation than while working if work is your crutch.

You are okay as long as you're on the job, sticking to a schedule, following directions, reaching goals and getting feedback. When the work stops, the cravings start. Vacations are unstructured voids. What can you do besides drink?

Sobriety is pointless if all you do is work. Recovery is about a fuller and richer life, not just a job. You don't live to work.

Vacations are meant to be fun. They're part of the payoff for getting your life back together. Make your holiday an opportunity to learn how to have fun again without drinking. You deserve it!

Your respite from work should be a gift you give yourself for staying sober, not a cause for slipping into relapse. Use your vacation to take your recovery to the next level. Stretch your sobriety a step beyond work. Take your vacation with no fear, no regrets and no booze. Use the steps below as your vacation planner.

Action Plan

- ► Don't just "take" your vacation time. Plan something worthwhile. (Lasting memories don't just happen.) Look forward to fulfilling the plan. The secret is to take a vacation *to* something, not just *from* something.
- ► Start with short vacations. Two weeks of fun and freedom may be more than you can handle at first.
- ► Keep up your AA rituals while on vacation. Read daily meditations. Attend AA meetings wherever you go.
- ► Choose carefully where you go, what you do and whom you do it with. Disney World is probably better than Las Vegas. Physical activity works better than passive pursuits for keeping your mind away from alcohol. Sober friends are safer companions than your old drinking buddies.
- ► Plan alcohol-free activities the whole family can enjoy. (See Appendix C.)
- ► Don't spend more than you can afford. You don't want to feel guilty. Guilt is a guest that won't leave and often brings relapse along with it.
- ► Don't take a halfhearted vacation. Resist calling or

49

checking in to work every day. You can't "get away" unless you really get away.

► Don't take a vacation from your recovery program. Keep in touch. Send a postcard to your sponsor.

► Lighten up. Stick to a reasonable regimen. Know your limits. Don't work harder at your vacation than you do at your job.

► Do things that strengthen your recovery:
1. Practice your relaxation skills.
2. Volunteer. Do something for others. Anonymous good deeds can do wonders for your self esteem.
3. Do some Twelfth Step work you normally don't have time for.
4. Read self-help and recovery literature. (See Appendix F.)
5. Take time to do all of the 12 steps right. Take personal inventory again. Concentrate on gratitude.
6. Go on a retreat.
7. Make conscious contact with your Higher Power.
8. Reward and pamper yourself. (See Appendix E.)

► Don't feel you have to take an exotic trip to have a good vacation. Sometimes, the best vacation is to do nothing and do it slowly. Use some time to relax, reflect, meditate and pray. If you can find some inner peace, you've come a long way in your recovery.

Trap #20 - Retirement

It's never too late for recovery and it's never too late for relapse. Each year, more and more senior citizens are revisiting old drinking problems. Often, the cause is retirement. For too many alcoholics, retirement, after an active life of working and contributing, is one of life's final relapse traps.

Retirement should be a time for reward and serenity. However, many people find it a time of isolation, irrelevance, loneliness, depression and heavy drinking. When people feel unwanted and unneeded, it's easy to revert to old patterns, habits and addictions. It's tragic when relapse reclaims someone after years of sobriety. Don't let it happen to you.

The secret to successful retirement is to have "something important yet to do." You're never too old to set new goals, renew old passions, develop new interests or start a new career. Look for a purpose–it is the key to a healthy and happy retirement and the secret to lasting sobriety.

Bookstores are full of self-help texts with retirement advice about finances, health care, housing and travel. If you're a senior citizen *and* a recovering alcoholic, what you really need is advice on how to stay sober. Retirement is a gift too good to lose. Savor the precious remaining years, don't blot them out with booze.

Eventually, retirement comes to most former drinkers. Relapse doesn't have to come with it. The guides below offer practical ways to avoid slips and stay sober during your golden years. Happy retirement. You've earned it!

51

Action Plan

- Use some of your new-found time to do recovery reading (i.e., the scriptures, the Big Book, etc.). (See Appendix F.)
- Stay in contact with sober people. AA groups for senior citizens and retirees are many. Join one (or more).
- Become a sponsor. You have the wisdom and experience to help someone else who is just starting on the long road to recovery.
- Consider yourself a role model. Show others, of all ages, that recovery works.
- Keep using self affirmations. You never outlive the need for positive self-talk. (See Appendix D.)
- Become active in your local senior citizen center. Help with the chemical health program.
- Stay healthy. Get periodic physical exams and follow your doctor's advice. (It won't include using alcohol as medication.)
- Write your memoirs or autobiography. Include your experiences with alcohol, the consequences and the wonder of recovery. Your story can be a lasting legacy to your children and grandchildren.
- Find comfort in poetry. (Both reading and writing it.)
- Keep your sense of humor. It's better to laugh than to drink.
- Now that you have the time, finish making amends to all those you've harmed. You want to leave a clean slate.
- Maintain relationships with children. It will help keep you young and sober.

- Start making a gratitude list. It may take years to complete.
- Don't vegetate–rest, eat, work, play, talk, exercise. Don't leave time in your life to think about drinking.
- Don't hesitate to ask for help at the first sign of trouble.
- Notice how your cravings have decreased over the years.
- Renew your commitment to sobriety. Write it down, sign it and read it to yourself often.
- Make burial and funeral plans. Get your affairs in order, including your will and a living will. You'll feel good about yourself. People who feel positive about themselves, at any age, don't need to hide behind a bottle.
- Recruit family members to be your watchdogs and report to you any early warning signs of depression or relapse they see. If any appear, get professional help.

SECTION III

SOCIAL TRAPS

Section III

SOCIAL TRAPS

The scariest part of recovery for many alcoholics is reconstructing a vibrant and satisfying social life. When your social relationships and leisure-time recreation have revolved around a bottle for most or all of your adult life, it's hard to visualize a social life without booze. Most recovering drunks can't imagine what they will do with their friends, their free time and themselves without drinking. They don't know how to have fun while sober and they're afraid to even try.

During the early stages of recovery, the social scene is like a mine field full of hazards that can blow up anytime destroying months of sobriety in a flash. Because you are all a little insecure, you're always most vulnerable in social settings where your behavior is on public display. Each social situation has its own set of singular tensions, temptations and tests which can wreck recovery. At first, it often seems as if every social event is a reason for relapse. It doesn't have to be that way.

There's no point to recovery if you can't take control of your social life and learn how to make friends, have fun and enjoy living free of alcohol. The secret is to go slow, seek effective guidance and have a plan for dealing with a variety of social pressures.

This section offers specific, real-world advice for handling the common social situations men and women new to sobriety are most afraid of; are most emotionally volatile; and are most likely to trigger a slip or relapse.

These survival tips can prepare you in advance for everyday public situations plus special social events and can provide the courage, confidence and competencies necessary to win back your social life.

These suggestions have worked for alcoholics of all ages and stages of recovery. They can work for you too. Dare to try them. You'll be surprised how much fun sobriety can be!

Trap #21 - Dating and the Single Scene

Most experts suggest alcoholics new to recovery avoid dating, having sex and/or developing serious relationships with the opposite sex until sobriety is well-established. This is sound (though hard-to-follow) advice. Inevitably, however, even recovering alcoholics have to get a life. If you're sober and single, you will start playing the dating game eventually. (Romance after recovery is possible!)

Meeting and dating new people is always scary. It's especially frightening when you are unsure of your self and your sobriety. Dating inevitably involves vulnerability, self-disclosure, risk-taking and the threat of rejection. It's no wonder so many people drink on dates. Fortunately, help is available.

During early recovery, don't rush relationships. When you're ready, try tested ways to handle the single scene, to enjoy dating and to reinvent a social life which includes sexual relationships-without risking relapse. The following action steps can help make it happen.

Action Plan

- Don't date too much too soon. You're the only one who knows when you're ready.
- Avoid dating known drinkers–including rekindling an old romance with someone who still drinks.
- Stay away from singles bars. Find alcohol-free places to meet new people. Try a church, a community education class, your favorite grocery store or a popular spa.
- Change your daily routine. It increases the opportunities to make and meet new friends.
- Attend AA meetings regularly. They provide support *and* new contacts.
- Remember how you acted on dates before you started drinking.
- Visualize dating without alcohol; then act out your vision.
- Stay close to your sponsor for advice, counsel and reality checks.
- Start with a breakfast or lunch date.
- Plan dates that feature fun without drinking. (See Appendix C.)
- Stick with restaurants and clubs that don't serve alcohol. (If it helps, insist on the nonsmoking section.)
- Be up-front about your recovery status. If a date is scared away by your sobriety, it wasn't a good match anyway.
- Double-date with sober friends.
- Simplify your life–especially your love life. Don't date more than one person at a time for a while.

- As with other things, take your dating one day at a time. Don't get too serious too soon.
- If things don't work out, don't try to drown your sorrows. They float. Remember, it's just the end of a relationship, not the end of your sobriety.

Trap #22 - Party Time

For most people, parties are fun. Recovering alcoholics may experience parties as a special kind of torture. Even the thought of a cocktail or office party can be painful and terrifying.

Attending social gatherings and functions where drinking is the norm and some people may expect you to drink can be a cruel test for anyone newly sober.

For many newcomers to recovery, parties are places where relapses become contagious. Many recovering alcoholics truly believe they will never be able to attend parties again. They think it is the price they have to pay for sobriety. They're wrong!

It's O.K. to be wary. However, sooner or later, you will have to go to some kind of party. Don't panic. Make proper preparation by rehearsing talk and behavior. With a plan in mind, you can survive any party, stay sober and even have fun. The precautions and proactive measures below can show you how.

Action Plan

- Visualize staying sober at the party.
- Talk it over with your sponsor in advance.

- Share your apprehensions and fears in AA
- .Practice "turn down" phrases ahead of time. (See Appendix B.)
- Be prepared for some bad jokes and/or ridicule.
- Boost your confidence with positive self talk. (See Appendix D.)
- Stay away if you truly feel you can't handle it.
- Take Antabuse (if prescribed).
- Attend the party with sober friends.
- Tell the host and bartender you aren't drinking.
- Order water, soda pop or juice. Sometimes, it helps to carry a glass around. (If nothing else, it gives you something to do with your hands.)
- Avoid smoking, coffee, salty treats or fried foods that may trigger cravings.
- Stay focused on why you're attending the party.
- Stay only a short time. Leave if you begin to feel uncomfortable.
- Remember why you quit drinking. (Play the whole tape in your mind, including all of the bad consequences you've experienced.)
- If you feel pressured, take a break and practice deep breathing.
- Reward yourself afterward. (See Appendix E.)

Trap #23 - Holidays

Holidays are stressful for everyone–especially alcoholics in recovery. No matter which holiday is being celebrated, there are always lots of parties, family gatherings, temptations and excesses of all kinds. Often, issues of loneliness, guilt, self-pity, past mistakes, missed opportunities and ruined relationships become magnified at holiday time.

It's common for people in our society to feel fatigued, stressed-out and depressed during holiday periods. That's why more relapses occur over holidays than at other times of the year. Recovery is always in jeopardy at holiday time. This doesn't mean you can't enjoy holidays and stay sober; it just means you have to plan ahead and keep your priorities straight.

It may not be easy to handle holidays without relapsing, but it is always possible. The following steps can help guide you through the hazards of holidays without a slip. Try them–they work. Happy holidays!

Action Plan

▸ Focus on the real meaning of the holiday.

▸ Use the opportunity to develop your spiritual life if it's a religious holiday–attend church, pray, read inspirational literature. Do whatever it takes to get in touch with your spiritual side.

▸ Remember what worked for you before alcohol took over.

▸ Visualize how you will get through the holidays without drinking.

▸ Limit attendance at holiday parties and follow other party survival tips (see Trap #22).

▸ Get plenty of rest and exercise. The better you feel, the less likely you are to slip or relapse.

▸ Pamper yourself. It's not selfishness–it's survival. (See Appendix E.)

- Make AA part of your holiday plans. Many AA groups hold special meetings immediately before, during and after all major holidays.
- Touch base with your sponsor. Holidays are no time to be alone.
- Limit time with relatives if family is part of your problem.
- Celebrate the holiday with people from AA whom you know and trust.
- Refuse to be a victim. Don't feel sorry for yourself.
- Build in quiet time for meditation and practicing relaxation techniques.
- Volunteer to help at a homeless shelter or a soup kitchen. Helping others is a sure-fire way to help yourself survive and enjoy any holiday.

Trap #24 - Deja Vu (Visiting Old Haunts & Old Cronies)

"Should auld acquaintance be forgot?" Probably. The last thing a recovering drunk needs is to hang out at a favorite watering hole "where everybody knows your name" with a bunch of old drinking buddies. Purposely testing yourself and your sobriety is high risk behavior. However, you can't always distance yourself from these all-too-familiar places and people.

Sometimes, circumstances require you to return to previous surroundings and friends. Sometimes, you just want to. In either case, being around old haunts and old cronies can be a powerful trigger for relapse. After all, drinking is the only way you've ever known how to act in these situations. To make matters worse, your sobriety may intimidate your old binge buddies creating even more tension and pressure. The only way to successfully reunite with your past life is to learn some new skills and behaviors.

Part of staying sober is starting a new life with some new surroundings, new friends and new activities. The best approach to sustained sobriety is to avoid old haunts and cronies until you're entirely ready. Then reenter your old world gradually. At the same time, build a new network of support and other elements of a new life. The next action plan shows you how.

Action Plan

- Stay away from your old drinking spots and your old "friends" for as long as you need to. You don't have to prove anything to anyone.
- If you do go, stay only a short while the first time or two.
- Listen to your instincts. When your gut tells you it's time to go–leave immediately.
- Take along a supportive (and sober) friend.
- Talk to your sponsor before you go.
- Be prepared for the flack you'll get from your friends who are still drinking.
- Plan ahead what you will talk about (what you'll say and how you'll say it).
- Practice turn-down phrases. (See Appendix B.)
- Keep in mind why you quit drinking.
- Touch base with your "powerlessness." Revisit Step 1 before you go.

- ▸ Boost your confidence with positive self talk. (See Appendix D.)
- ▸ Practice being assertive.
- ▸ Be willing to talk about your treatment and recovery but don't preach.
- ▸ Reward yourself afterward. (See Appendix E.)
- ▸ Always balance the time you spend with former cronies with an equal amount of time spent with people from your new life. It's important to keep in mind the fun, friends and purpose of sobriety.
- ▸ Change your routine (what you do, where you go and when you do it). This helps differentiate your old life from your new one.
- ▸ Do whatever it takes to make new friends. Attending AA meetings is a good start.
- ▸ Try new things and find new ways to have fun. (See Appendix C.)
- ▸ Don't dwell on the past–focus on the future. (Memories can be seductive.) Fill your mind with plans, hopes, dreams and goals to be achieved. Take one day at a time. Some day, old haunts and cronies will be less important. They may even fade out of your life completely.

Trap #25 - Breakups

No matter how careful you are, bad things can happen–even to good relationships. Breakups occur in everyone's life. When it happens to someone in recovery, the impact is particularly devastating because it opens up old issues of insecurity, self doubt and self worth. If a legitimate reason for a relapse exists, the unraveling of a meaningful relationship might be it.

Breakups are like deaths. They leave the affected parties feeling angry, betrayed, alone, vulnerable and, often, hopeless. This is dangerous territory for a drunk trying to stay clean and sober.

A breakup with someone very close to you isn't the end of the world of course, but it can be the end of your sobriety if you allow it. *Don't allow it.*

Every breakup can be the beginning of something new, perhaps something better. Follow the recipe for rebounding from a breakup and staying sober in the process by using the following steps.

Action Plan

- Let grief happen. It's okay to feel anger and denial. The grieving process is essential to healing.
- Don't believe you have to feel guilty, ashamed or sorry for yourself. Breakups don't have to be anybody's fault.
- Keep your life simple for a while. Don't rush into another relationship. One day at a time applies.
- Try to learn from the event and go on with your life.
- Ask yourself, "Will drinking make anything better?" Remember, sorrows don't drown.
- Avoid places, people and events that trigger painful memories of the broken relationship.
- Keep busy. Take on extra responsibility at work or immerse yourself in a hobby.
- Use this opportunity to take personal inventory. What do you need to work on to become the person

you want to be?

- Spend time with your sponsor and other AA friends.
- Attend AA meetings and talk about your feelings.
- Get lots of exercise and rest.
- Try church and prayer again. Don't breakup with your Higher Power.
- Keep a journal. Writing is therapeutic.
- If depression persists, get a medical evaluation. Clinical depression can become deadly.
- Focus on what's going right in your life. Take time for gratitude. You are most likely better off than you think you are.

Trap #26 - Sporting Events

Sports are part of social life in America. Unfortunately, sports have become closely linked with booze. Sports and drinking go together in our society.

Beer, wine and liquor companies sponsor sporting events. Sports stadiums and arenas sell alcoholic beverages. Sports heroes become spokespersons for alcohol products. People drink before sporting events to get revved up for the big game. People drink while watching sporting events and people drink to celebrate the victory of a favorite team or to dull the agony of defeat.

Sports are fun but the party atmosphere that often accompanies sporting events can trigger relapse. Recovering alcoholics don't have to abandon sports. However, it pays to take certain steps to keep your sobriety in shape while participating in sports and/or attending or watching sporting events. Here's a suggested sobriety fitness program.

Action Plan

- ▶ Stay away from sporting events until you're sure you can handle the circus-like climate.
- ▶ Follow the same survival tips suggested for other parties. (See Trap #22.)
- ▶ Skip tailgating events.
- ▶ Watch sporting events from bars or clubs that do not serve alcohol.
- ▶ Attend with sober friends or invite them to watch with you at home.
- ▶ Remember how you enjoyed sporting events before you started drinking.
- ▶ Notice how many other spectators are not drinking. Also notice how obnoxiously intoxicated fans behave. It's one of the best arguments for sobriety.
- ▶ If you're tempted to imbibe, recall all the bad consequences you've experienced.
- ▶ Remember it's only a game.
- ▶ Find alternative ways to celebrate (i.e., Start "the wave," form a conga line, break out the ice cream, etc.).
- ▶ Reward yourself for not drinking. (See Appendix E.)

Trap #27 - Pre-Wedding Parties

All parties can place sobriety at risk. Bachelor and single woman parties are particularly perilous for recovering alcoholics.

The whole purpose of these admittedly hedonistic celebrations is to create an off-the-wall, anything goes, last fling atmosphere. Alcohol is usually a staple. Dancers (often strippers) commonly provide the entertainment and lewd, irresponsible behavior is often encouraged. This is not a supportive environment for a fragile sobriety.

Of course, you don't have to attend if you don't approve of such parties. However, if you do go, the following tips can help you participate, enjoy and survive with your sobriety intact.

Action Plan

- Suggest that the host plan wholesome fun and serve non-alcoholic beverages.
- Attend an AA meeting before going to the party.
- Follow the suggestions for other parties. (See Trap #22.)
- Plan to stay only a short time. Leave immediately if the party gets out of hand.
- Attend with sober friends.
- Volunteer to be the designated driver.
- Tell the guest of honor in advance why you won't be drinking.
- Notice how many other people present are not drinking. If they can do it, so can you.

- Concentrate on food, not drink.
- Always act as if your behavior is being videotaped. (It might be.)
- Remember. The party is a prelude to a much more important event--a wedding. Don't do anything that might taint this special occasion.
- Keep your sobriety uppermost in your mind. Don't throw away weeks or months of recovery for a few moments of madness.
- Reward yourself later for staying sober. (See Appendix E.)

Trap #28 - Weddings

Not all weddings showcase free drinks and champagne toasts, but many do. They may pressure you to join in if you attend a wedding where drinking is prevalent,

It seems innocent enough. How much harm can a few good-natured toasts to the bride and groom do? The answer is, plenty! Relapses begin this way.

You may think it is easier to go along with the crowd rather than to risk embarrassment by standing out as a teetotaler especially if your sobriety is shaky. You need to remember–and keep telling yourself–your drinking or not drinking can't make or break any wedding party. No wedding reception is a good enough reason to sacrifice your recovery. Use the suggestions below to help you get through any wedding without crossing the line and without crashing in the punchbowl.

Action Plan

- Don't go if you feel you can't resist the temptation.
- Skip the reception if necessary.
- Follow the survival tips for other parties. (See Trap #22.)
- Stick with nondrinkers.
- Practice turn-down phrases beforehand. (See Appendix B.)
- Eat a lot of wedding cake. It suppresses the urge to drink alcohol.
- Make toasts using water or soda.
- Notice all the other people present who aren't drinking. Do what they do.
- Focus on the newlyweds, not on yourself.
- Tell your server in advance not to pour you any champagne.
- If they have music at the reception, dance–a lot. Physical activity helps keep you from drinking.
- Make your abstinence a special gift to the newlyweds. They don't need a noisy drunk disrupting their most sacred occasion.
- Reward yourself when it's all over and you have dodged the bullet. (See Appendix E.)

Trap #29 - Concerts

It's hard to think of a worse place for a recently recovered alcoholic than a rock concert. Booze and pot are everywhere and the mood is crazy.

If you have to go, remember not everyone at the concert is high, it only seems that way. You can be one of the clearheaded ones. Follow these directions to enjoy the music without the mood-altering accompaniments.

Action Plan

- Choose your bands carefully. Some groups draw wilder crowds and provoke more insane behavior than others.
- Go to an AA meeting first. Talk about your apprehensions and promise to report back later.
- Ask your Higher Power to help you get through the evening without a slip.
- Go with friends who love music, but don't drink.
- Expect to get some flack from the regulars.
- Be assertive about abstinence.
- Keep repeating AA slogans to bolster your conviction.
- Count how many people you notice who aren't stoned or drunk.
- Revisit your first step. Remember what "powerlessness" means.
- Focus on the music.
- Fill up on pop and water.
- Hold on to your sobriety medallion. Rub it as a reminder of your recovery. It can be your anchor to reality.
- Don't delude yourself into thinking that a joint might be O.K. as long as you don't drink. Recovery requires abstinence from all addictive substances.
- Leave at the intermission if cravings begin to make you feel uncomfortable.
- Reward yourself afterward. (See Appendix E.)

Trap #30 - Travel With Friends (Plane, Train or Champagne)

An aura of excitement, adventure and recklessness surrounds traveling. This can be especially true if you travel with friends who like to drink. If you go by train or plane, the drinks may be cheap or, even, free. A much better setup for slipping or relapsing is hard to find.

When you're traveling with friends, it's easy to let your guard down but it's always a bad idea. Follow the suggested travel guidelines below instead.

Action Plan

- If everyone going on the trip drinks, consider staying home or inviting at least one sober friend to accompany you.
- Talk to your sponsor before you leave home.
- Ask your Higher Power to travel with you.
- Plan ahead of time what to talk about to help pass the time.
- Practice turn-down phrases in advance. (See Appendix B.)
- Use positive self talk to prepare yourself for the trip. (See Appendix D.)
- Stick close to the nondrinkers in the crowd.
- Keep busy during the trip. (Enjoy the scenery, read, work puzzles, take a nap, etc.)
- Order only water, soda, coffee or tea
- Eat a lot, but avoid salty food.

- If you're tempted to drink, practice deep breathing and repeat AA affirmations.
- Concentrate on the fun you can have on the trip without drinking. Check ahead of time on the alcohol-free events and activities available at your destination.
- Before you leave, request a list of alcohol-free restaurants from the Chamber of Commerce or Bureau of Tourism at your destination.
- Plan your trip's activities and daily schedules ahead of time. Don't leave too much to chance. Sobriety requires structure during the early stages.
- Remember, an AA group is always available wherever you go in the civilized (and not so civilized) world.
- Keep in touch with your sponsor and home AA group while traveling.

Trap #31 - Class Reunions

Class reunions are always highly charged with emotion. They are one of the few social events without a single guest of honor–everyone is high profile at a class reunion.

Most people have mixed emotions about attending. They're eager to relive past memories, to catch up on what's happened since graduation and to reconnect with old friends. They're also concerned about their appearance, apprehensive about their aging, embarrassed by the limitations of their achievements, and worried about how their lives will stack up against those of their former classmates. It's no surprise people drink a lot at class reunions.

Alcoholics in recovery may feel especially sensitive, insecure and self-conscious at reunions. They're afraid old friends may think less of them because of their alcoholism.

Class reunions are world class relapse traps. Never attend a reunion of classmates without making thorough preparations. The action plan which follows can help you stay on track and out of trouble at reunion time.

Action Plan

- Don't go if you can't get comfortable with the situation.
- Visualize how you will behave at the reunion.
- Plan what you will talk about and how much self-disclosure you can handle.
- Practice turn-down phrases in advance. (See Appendix B.)
- Stop by an AA meeting on the way to the reunion.
- Bring a supportive friend.
- Stay only a short time if you're uncomfortable.
- Stop yourself from any negative self talk.
- Look your best! It will give you greater confidence.
- Force yourself to be assertive.
- Use the opportunity to make amends with former classmates.
- Make the reunion a new beginning by forgiving others (and yourself).

- Be sure you know which punchbowl is spiked.
- Concentrate on not taking that first drink.
- Remind yourself that one out of every ten of your former classmates is likely to be an alcoholic too.
- Maintain your perspective. You don't have to prove anything to these people anymore.
- Give yourself a major reward for surviving the reunion. (See Appendix E.)

Trap #32 - Conflict Situations

Even in our violent society, most people dislike conflict. Yet, arguments and disagreements are inevitable in everyone's social life. No matter how mellow you try to be, eventually you will have some kind of conflict with an acquaintance or friend. When your social life turns nasty, the likelihood of a slip or relapse increases dramatically.

People who drink often settle their arguments with force or physical violence. As someone who wants to stay sober, you have to learn ways to settle disputes peacefully.

Conflicts cause tensions and tensions can cause people to drink. Minimizing and managing conflict situations are essential to maintaining sobriety. When conflicts arise in your social life, here's what to do about it.

Action Plan

- Avoid people and places associated with conflicts in your life.
- Spend time with AA members. Conflicts seldom break out at AA meetings.
- Exercise to work off anger and emotion.
- Pray for a peaceful solution to each new conflict situation. The Serenity Prayer is a powerful antidote for anger.
- Take a break or walk away from a conflict-in-the-making.
- Practice meditation and relaxation techniques to reduce hostility.
- Discuss the problem with your sponsor or AA group.
- Face your disputant and talk about the problem. Be honest about your feelings.
- Practice active listening. Be sure you hear what the other person in the conflict is saying. Often, you're not as far apart as you think you are.
- Avoid using put-downs, blaming and name-calling.
- Work with the other disputant to identify alternative solutions to the conflict. Evaluate the pros and cons of each remedy.
- Agree on the best mutually acceptable solution.
- Commit to doing your part to end the controversy.

Trap #33 - Bets and Dares

It's always open season on recovering alcoholics. Old cronies, still drinking, delight in baiting reformed drunks with bets and dares in hopes of toppling them off the wagon. Sometimes, it works. Unfortunately, false pride, embarrassment, old-fashioned ego and/or the macho mystique make it hard for some people to resist this kind of peer pressure.

Don't let anyone con you out of your sobriety. If so-called "friends" persist in trying to coax you into drinking with bets or dares, here's how to handle it.

Action Plan

- Ask your sponsor and AA friends how they handle bets and dares.
- Ignore the proposition—walk away. Never take a bet or dare that involves drinking.
- Always have a sober friend close by.
- Change the stakes. Substitute something which doesn't involve drinking.
- Be prepared to get plenty of flack from your drinking "friends."
- Do your best to be assertive.
- Remember that your real friends want you to remain sober.
- Bolster your resolve through positive self talk. (See Appendix D.)

- Remember why you quit drinking and keep your priorities straight. Don't risk recovery over a stupid wager or dare. It's better to lose a bet than to sacrifice your sobriety.
- Dare to be a "chicken." After all, there's nothing macho about relapse.
- Use humor to defuse the situation.
- If necessary, ask the manager, bartender or bouncer to tell your challenger to "cool it" and quit bothering you.
- Reward yourself big time after you've dodged the bullet.

Trap #34 - Loss of a Friend

A loss can be painful and difficult. The loss of a close friend through moving, death or other means is particularly devastating. It leaves a gaping hole in your life and you feel alone and vulnerable. These are not good omens for maintaining sobriety.

Times of loss are easy times to start drinking again. It doesn't help, but sometimes, it's the only way you know to dull the pain.

Don't fall into this relapse trap. You can use better ways to deal with the void and stay sober at the same time. These few action steps really work.

Action Plan

- Share your loss with your sponsor and your AA group.
- Fall back on your spiritual life. Try church again. Pray, starting with the Serenity Prayer and the Lord's Prayer.
- Practice distraction–stay busy.
- Write down your feelings.
- Cherish memories of happier moments in your friendship and move on. You can't thrive on memories alone.
- Step up your exercise program.
- Don't count on alcohol to fill the void. It can only add to your pain.
- Develop new relationships. New friendships don't dishonor old ones.
- Remember what you liked most about your friend and try to incorporate those qualities into your own life. It's a special way to pay tribute to your friend and your friendship.
- Do what you would want your friend to do if you were the one who was absent or departed.
- Remember that your friend would not want you to use this loss as an excuse to start drinking again.

Trap #35 - Drinks On the House

There's no such thing as free lunch and there's *really* no such thing as free drinks. The cost of free booze is too high for any recovering alcoholic.

Any social event (i.e., open house, grand opening, rush party, etc.) featuring free drinks is a disaster area for people newly sober. Attending such affairs is almost like volunteering for a relapse.

The best advice is to stay away. If you have to go, however, here are the steps to follow.

Action Plan

- Visualize yourself getting through the event without drinking.
- Practice turn-down phrases in advance. (See Appendix B.)
- Be prepared for negative reactions from other people present.
- Stick with supportive friends.
- Find out which non-alcoholic drinks are available. Soft drinks or coffee are always obtainable somewhere.
- Don't stay any longer than you have to.
- Bolster your resolve by reciting AA slogans and positive self talk. (See Appendix D.)
- Carry an AA medallion to remind you of where you have been and where you are now.
- Have a plan for what you want to do afterwards.

Give yourself a reason to look forward to leaving.

- Stay as far away from the bar as possible. Schmooze on the other side of the room or hall.

- Kill time in the restroom or take a tour of the premises–whatever it takes to pass the time without drinking.

- Keep busy. Mingle. Help pick up dirty glasses or empty ashtrays. Don't give yourself time to feel awkward or to think about drinking.

- Get out of yourself. Concentrate on other people. Really listen to others' conversations. It will boost your popularity and help keep you sober, too.

- Realize that most people present are more interested in getting all the free drinks they can than they are in whether you're drinking or not. You're the center of attention in your own mind only. What you do will go largely unnoticed. Staying sober is easier than you might think.

- Give yourself a reward equal to the amount of pressure you've withstood.

SECTION IV

PHYSICAL TRAPS

Section IV

PHYSICAL TRAPS

"If you ruin your body, where will you live?"

- Anon.

Relapse traps can be physical as well as mental and emotional. Sometimes, our own bodies betray us. Any illness, injury or other real or imagined physical problem can make a sober alcoholic more susceptible to relapse.

When you feel lousy, it's hard to maintain the strength, the energy and the will to resist urges and temptations. On the other hand, it's easy to feel weak, vulnerable and confused. Relapse thrives on such conditions.

Many alcoholics start drinking to feel euphoric and end up drinking just to feel normal. It's only natural, then, for drunks to turn to booze to make them feel better when they're physically ill or off balance. Treating aches and pains with liquor is tempting. It doesn't work but alcoholics are slow learners. Physical frailty or affliction increases the likelihood of a slip or a full relapse.

Of course, if you wait until you're perfectly fit and healthy to get sober, it will never happen. Inevitably you have to get past the physical relapse traps that stand in the way if recovery is going to come about.

This section prescribes common remedies for some of the most common physical conditions that are conducive to relapse. It starts by dealing with the physical symptoms of withdrawal.

Trap #36 - Withdrawal

"I was shipwrecked before I got aboard."

Seneca the Younger

Recovery is over before it begins for some alcoholics–they can't get past the withdrawal. Unable to take the pain and discomfort, they cave in quickly and go back to booze. It takes resolve and courage to withstand the physical agonies of withdrawal. Unless the alcoholic is entirely ready, it won't happen.

Withdrawal is never pretty and it can be torture. Although individual cases differ, symptoms frequently include tremors (the "shakes"), alternating chills and sweats, cramps, spasms, dizziness, retching, diarrhea, disorientation, hallucinations, delusions, nervousness, and insomnia. Withdrawal isn't easy but it's not supposed to be. It's recovery's first major test.

Surviving the physical reactions to the sudden absence of alcohol from the body can be deadly serious business. It's a battle at best. If you win, you get your life back!

Since withdrawal can be dangerous, don't take it lightly–plan for it. Before taking your "last drink," get a physical evaluation from a certified counselor or physician to decide if you should check into a detox center, clinic, treatment facility or hospital during withdrawal. In extreme cases, withdrawal can be life-threatening unless carefully monitored by chemical health specialists or health care professionals. Don't take chances. The first phase of recovery is the wrong time to die of alcoholism.

First, get medical clearance to detox on your own without being confined under constant medical supervision Then, the coping strategies below can help get you through the withdrawal process without relapse. It's a victory worth winning. It will change your life forever. Go for it!

Action Plan

- Follow your doctor's and counselor's orders to the letter. Don't try to prove how tough you are. There's a difference between bravery and foolish bravado.
- Talk to other alcoholics who have gone through withdrawal. What was like it? What helped?
- Clear your calendar and make arrangements to be on the sideline for several days. Ridding your body of residual alcohol takes time. Don't try to rush the process.
- Don't go through withdrawal alone.
- Create a safe and sterile environment for your withdrawal. No booze. No ads for booze. Not even a matchbook cover from a bar.
- Announce your intent in advance. The more people who know what you're attempting, the more difficult it is for you to give up.
- Be mentally prepared for the long haul. Expect it to be bad. Expect it to get better.
- Take withdrawal one *hour* at a time.
- Minimize the use of sedatives, tranquilizers and sleeping pills. Don't confuse substituting chemicals for real recovery.
- Don't try to stop smoking while you are detoxing.

One withdrawal at a time is enough.

- Keep in touch with your sponsor the whole time.
- Pray–a lot. It helps!
- Let your sober friends support you. Frequent visits and lots of hugs mean a lot and make a difference.
- Eat right. Exercise. Sleep as much as you can. It's not too early to start living a healthy life.
- Keep busy. Work the 12 steps. Read self-help literature (See Appendix F). Keep an hour-by-hour journal. A record of your journey may help others later.
- Practice deep breathing and drink lots of water. The quicker you cleanse your system the better.
- Write down all your reasons for not drinking. Post the list. Refer to it often during withdrawal.
- When you're feeling your worst, remove yourself psychologically–"leave the field." Daydream, fantasize. There's more to recovery than just reality.
- Stay focused on your goal of life free from alcohol. What you're going through now is called "making it happen."
- No matter how hard it gets, hang on a little longer. Wait out the cravings.
- When it's over, CELEBRATE big time. Reward yourself. The first test is the hardest.

Trap #37 - Illness

Sickness interrupts work, play and daily routines; but it doesn't have to interrupt recovery. Alcoholics are like everyone else when they get sick. They feel down, depressed, defenseless, weak, vulnerable and sorry for themselves. What more could a relapse-in-waiting ask for?

Illness during early sobriety is particularly threatening to recovery. It makes it harder to get to meetings or to stick to a 12-step program. It's tempting to consider postponing sobriety until you feel better. Don't! It pays to separate alcoholism from other unrelated illnesses.

Keep in mind that when you're sick, you're not yourself. Your guard is down and you're not thinking clearly. These conditions can easily set you up for a slip, unless you take extra precautions.

Use the steps below to build a coping plan. They won't cure the common cold but they can keep your sobriety on track until you get over whatever is ailing you. Take as directed!

Action Plan

- ▸ Be sure to tell your doctor you're a recovering alcoholic. It may make a difference in what drugs or medications are prescribed for your condition.
- ▸ Follow your doctor's orders explicitly. Finish taking any prescription. Don't get up before you get your physician's okay. Following directions will speed healing. The quicker you get well, the sooner you can get on with your recovery.
- ▸ If you use over-the-counter medications, be sure they're alcohol-free. Your pharmacist can help you find them.
- ▸ Be sure there's no booze around. You don't want to

tempt yourself when you're in a weakened condition or run the risk of grabbing the wrong bottle when you're feverish.

▸ Don't let anyone fix you a hot toddy or give you their grandmother's favorite "honey and whiskey" cold remedy. For a recovering alcoholic, there's no such thing as using liquor for medicinal purposes.

▸ Don't be alone for too long a period when you're ill. It's too easy to start brooding or thinking about drinking. Some company–sober company–can help keep your spirits up.

▸ When you're down, there's no better time to build yourself up with positive self-talk. Keep reciting your favorite affirmations. (See Appendix D.) They work even when you're lying down.

▸ Keep in touch with AA friends. Most AA groups issue a phone list. Use it.

▸ Use your down time to read, study, meditate and listen to recovery tapes.

▸ Resist cravings. Remember how many times alcohol has made you sick. How often did it ever make you well?

▸ Make some exciting plans for what you're going to do when you get well–plans that don't include alcohol.

Trap #38 - Pain

1. Pain makes people desperate.
2. Desperate people don't think straight.
3. Alcohol dulls pain.

No one knows these three things better than an alcoholic. Likewise, no one has a lower threshold for pain or a greater desire for quick fixes than an alcoholic. That's what makes physical pain one of the most powerful and seductive relapse traps of all.

When people are hurting, they want to be fixed and they don't care too much about whom or what does the fixing. It's no wonder, then, that a drink (or two or ten) looks extremely good to a sober drunk who is suffering with pain.

The problem is that alcohol not only deadens pain, it causes pain. To make matters worse, the pain produced by alcohol is contagious and relentless. It affects everyone you touch and it permeates every facet of your life. Compared to the agonies of chronic alcoholism, most other physical pain is an also-ran. When the trade off is between pain and sobriety, take sobriety every time.

Obviously, it takes strength, maturity, tenacity and courage to withstand pain and resist relapse. These are the same qualities necessary to achieve lasting sobriety under any condition. Fortunately, most pain is short-lived. However, even when it isn't, living with pain without trying to drown it in liquor is possible.

Making the pain go away isn't always possible but there are ways to make it bearable without resorting to alcohol as a painkiller. Experienced pain counselors and chemical dependency specialists alike recommend the action steps below as survival tools for living with pain–without alcohol.

Action Plan

- Meditate and pray often. Turn things over to your Higher Power. Pray for strength, not pity. Ask God the tough questions. Accept the answers.
- Watch which painkillers you take. Many are addictive. This isn't the time to acquire any more dependencies.
- Practice relaxation techniques. Sometimes, deep breathing exercises can be temporary pain relievers.
- Focus on the pain alcohol has caused you and others. It can put your other pain in perspective and remind you why you never want to drink again no matter how badly it hurts.
- Groan if you want to; curse if you must. Try not to whine. Groaning makes you feel better. Whining only makes you feel worse.
- Stay calm and keep busy. Work, play, go to AA meetings. Act as if you don't have time for pain.
- Revisit your gratitude list. You're better off than you think you are.
- Think of others. Undertake some Twelfth Step work. Helping others takes your mind away from your pain.
- Remove yourself psychologically. Visualize yourself some place where there isn't any pain.
- Whistle. Sing. Defy the hurting. Sometimes, you can fool your pain for a while.
- Enjoy humor. Laughter has healing properties.
- Read inspirational literature about successful people who have overcome pain.
- Pamper yourself with massages, bubble baths and other rewards that help soothe the pain for a little

while. (See Appendix E.)

▸ Consider alternative medical treatment for your pain, i.e., chiropractic, acupuncture, hypnosis, etc.

▸ Join a pain support group, seek pain counseling or get specialized pain treatment. (Some clinics and centers specialize exclusively in the treatment of pain.)

▸ Surround yourself with supportive people (family, AA friends, sponsors, etc.). When pain is your only companion, it dominates the relationship. When others are around, it has to compete for your attention.

Trap #39 - Fatigue and Sleep Deprivation

Fatigue, like illness, lowers defenses and heightens susceptibility to temptation and pressure. When people are over tired, they often feel lightheaded, disoriented, woozy and confused. They are more prone to poor judgment and unclear thinking. Fatigue tends to magnify problems and blur the lines between fantasy and reality. These are not the optimum conditions for remaining clean and sober. The risk of relapse is always greater when you're deprived of sleep or unusually tired.

Of course, fatigue can occur anytime during recovery. It is always a threat to sobriety and can be a health hazard. Extreme exhaustion may even become life-threatening. Fatigue is most formidable as a relapse trap, however, during the early stages of sobriety.

Unfortunately, it's fairly common for drunks starting recovery to push too hard, to overdo things, to lose sleep, to suffer from insomnia and/or literally wear themselves out. This happens for many reasons:

1. Body adjustments during withdrawal can cause insomnia.
2. After being drugged for most of their adult life, it's hard for recovering alcoholics to sleep naturally.
3. Cravings can make it difficult to rest or sleep.
4. Flashbacks and nightmares may interrupt sleep.
5. Many alcoholics have forgotten how to relax without booze.
6. The rush (natural high) and excitement of a new life can make it difficult to "come down" long enough to get needed rest.
7. Some alcoholics get caught up in a frenzy of recovery activities trying to make up for lost time. (We've all known people who have become fanatic in their recovery. They have exhausted themselves by attending three or four or more AA meetings every day. They spend long hours reading and working the 12-steps, making amends to everyone all at once and trying to live a "normal" life at the same time.)

Any of these causes or actions can facilitate fatigue and short-circuit sobriety. Recovery requires realistic thinking, awareness, energy, alertness and stamina. Fatigue undermines all of them.

"H.A.L.T." is a red flag acronym used within AA. It stands for being Hungry, Angry, Lonely and TIRED. Extra precautions are called for whenever any of these conditions exist. One of the things newcomers to sobriety have to watch out for is letting themselves get too tired.

Avoiding fatigue sounds easy–just rest.

Unfortunately, it isn't always that simple. It is possible,though, by sticking to the action plan outlined below. Try it.

Action Plan

- ▸ Focus on the Serenity Prayer. Repeat it often and do what it says. Turning over the things that you can't control is the key to finding peace–and rest.
- ▸ Simplify your life. The more complicated your existence is, the more tiring it is. Don't try to be superman or superwoman. "One day at a time" means just that!
- ▸ Stay away from sedatives and sleeping pills unless prescribed by a doctor. Adding more chemicals to the body is counterproductive for most recovering alcoholics.
- ▸ Establish a regular routine of waking and sleeping. The mind and body respond to rituals.
- ▸ Adopt a healthy lifestyle. Exercise and eat right. Stick with it, give it time to work. Your body can't return to its natural sleep patterns overnight.
- ▸ Work on your worries. For example, if money matters are keeping you awake, do something about them. Make a budget and stick to it. Spend less than you make. Don't buy what you can't afford. Consult a financial planner. The more personal problems you resolve, the less you have to lose sleep over.
- ▸ Ask other recovering alcoholics how they handle sleeplessness or fatigue. You'll get some much needed support and, maybe, some good suggestions as well.

- Practice relaxation techniques, such as deep breathing exercises, visualization, listening to quiet music or nature sounds on tape, etc. In the short term, a good rest is almost as good as sleep.
- Cut back on nicotine and caffeine.
- Try napping. Try not napping. Whatever works.
- Make a habit of repeating calming AA phrases such as K.I.S.S.–Keep It Simple Stupid; Let go and let God; Accept, don't expect; one day at a time. Internalizing these messages can help you to accept serenity and get some real rest.
- When you're really tired, let your sponsor and other sober friends do your clear thinking for you. Talk to them before you take that first drink.
- Establish a quiet time for prayer and meditation just before going to bed each night.
- If you can't get to sleep, get up and do something constructive. You can't force sleep. Just let it happen.
- If fatigue persists, seek medical help. Some clinics specialize in the treatment of sleep disorders and chronic fatigue syndrome (CFS).

Trap #40 - Light Deprivation (Seasonal Affective Disorder–S.A.D.)

Sunlight is a primary source of life and energy. Without it, people can become physically sick. Most people feel a little "let down" during prolonged periods without sunlight.

The problem is much worse for some people. These

individuals are particularly susceptible to the ill effects of light deprivation. They suffer from a variety of symptoms when denied exposure to sunlight for a long time. The problem is most frequent among people who live in cloudy, rainy or wintry climates. Doctors now label the condition, Seasonal Affective Disorder (S.A.D.) or Seasonal Depression.

Often, those suffering from light deprivation don't understand what's the matter with them but they know something is definitely wrong. When these people also happen to be recovering alcoholics, conditions may be ripe for a relapse.

Victims of light deprivation commonly describe the way they feel as lethargic, apathetic, listless, dumpy, depressed, uninterested, unmotivated and even numb. Their lives may be on hold. Their goals are no longer important. They "don't care" anymore. If that doesn't make you want a drink, what will? Obviously, these are some of the same warning signs that often signal a slip about to happen.

Maintaining sobriety is hard enough under any circumstances. If a recovering alcoholic also suffers from S.A.D. or light deprivation, it can be doubly difficult–but it *can* be done. Feeling the ill-effects of light deprivation isn't a good enough reason to start drinking again. If you're looking for a good excuse to drink, this isn't it. People get sober and stay sober every day, with or without sunlight. You can, too.

Follow the suggestions below if light deprivation is making life difficult for you. They won't bring back the sunlight but they can help you cope successfully without sunlight (temporarily) or alcohol (permanently). Even

without the sun, staying sober can be a day-brightener all
by itself.

Action Plan

▸ Take the problem of light deprivation seriously.
Admit it. Name it so you can deal with it. Tell others
(especially your sponsor and your boss) about your
problem. The more it's out in the open, the easier it
is to cope with.

▸ Use sun lamps or other special lamps (light boxes)
and reflectors which are now available to help
counteract the bad effects of light deprivation.

▸ Open up your house or apartment to let in as much of
the available light as possible.

▸ Spend as much time out-of-doors as you can.

▸ Join a support group for people who suffer from
S.A.D. Sometimes, just an AA group isn't enough.

▸ Take winter vacations or arrange weekend getaways
to sunnier climes.

▸ Don't resort to using artificial stimulants or other
mood-altering substances. They will only bring you
a step closer to slipping.

▸ Compensate for the lack of lift from sunlight by
praying more, increasing your recovery reading,
spending more time on the 12-steps, working harder
at pampering yourself (See Appendix E) and having
fun (See Appendix C).

▸ Surround yourself with upbeat people. Attend more
AA meetings during the winter months or the rainy
season.

▸ Buoy yourself up with positive self-talk (See

Appendix D).
- Fulfill your obligations even when you feel lethargic and unmotivated. You'll feel even worse if you fall behind at work or start letting people down.
- Seek medical help if needed.
- If things get too bad, consider moving to a place where the sun shines year-round. It's worth it if that's what it takes to stay sober.

Trap #41 - Clinical Depression

Clinical depression is a silent stalker that commonly goes undiagnosed for long periods. So is alcoholism.

Clinical depression is a progressive disease which robs sufferers of the ability to function in the most basic areas of life. So is alcoholism.

Undetected and untreated, clinical depression is a killer. So is alcoholism.

The similarities don't end there. Many of the warning signs for both diseases are essentially the same. Such as:

- Family history of the illness
- Inability to work or concentrate
- Apathy
- Mood swings
- Forgetfulness
- Fatigue
- Social Withdrawal
- Appetite loss
- Reduced sex drive
- Sleeplessness

Victims of both alcoholism and depression frequently feel overwhelmed and emotionally exhausted. They're unable to "snap out of it" by themselves. Ultimately, they often take their own lives.

Worse yet, the diseases feed on each other. People sometimes drink because they are depressed. Conversely, people may become depressed because they drink. Even dry drunks may suffer from depression if they don't change their attitudes and behaviors after getting sober.

Everyone experiences some periodic minor depression due to everyday setbacks, crises and problems. When the depression becomes prolonged and interferes with work, friendships and/or family relationships, it can wreck your recovery, cause you to relapse and it can kill you.

Clinical depression may be the most dangerous physical relapse trap of all for alcoholics just beginning recovery and for those with years of sobriety as well.

The good news is that depression is now treatable and controllable. There's no reason anymore for anyone to suffer in silence from major depression–not even a sober drunk.

Don't take chances with depression. If you experience prolonged feelings of hopelessness or helplessness, a drink won't help but the action steps below can. Try them. You can't afford not to.

Action Plan

▸ Learn as much as you can about clinical depression. Understanding the disease is your best defense.

- Monitor your moods and your physical well-being. The symptoms of major depression are sometimes masked as physical disorders, such as headaches or backaches.
- Talk about your negative feelings. Tell your family, your sponsor and your AA friends how you feel. If depression persists, talk to a health professional.
- Don't think that clinical depression will go away by itself. It won't. Recognize that your depression is an illness. It's okay to feel depressed. It's not okay to feel guilty or ashamed about it.
- Practice daily prayer and meditation. The Lord's Prayer and the Serenity Prayer are powerful antidepressants.
- Rediscover your church and your faith. You can find hope there.
- Ask your family and sober friends to pray for you. Research shows that it works.
- Stay connected. Physical and mental activities (i.e., games, puzzles, reading and exercise) can be antidotes for anxiety.
- Spend time with people who are supportive and understanding. Attend more meetings than usual. It's hard to be depressed in an AA group.
- Establish a pattern of using daily self-affirmations. (See Appendix D.) Convince yourself you can beat alcoholism and depression.
- Get lots of hugs. They really do help.
- Conduct a personal inventory, focusing on your strengths and what's going right. You're better off than you think you are. You still have lots to live for *and* to stay sober for.

- Maintain normal relationships and social contacts. Depression thrives on loneliness and isolation.
- Remind yourself that alcohol is a *depressant*. It can't help you. It can only make things worse.
- Ask those close to you for regular feedback, including any signs of progress or any signs of suicidal tendencies.
- Call your sponsor or an emergency hot line whenever you feel yourself slipping–especially if you're thinking about suicide.
- "Wait-A-Day." If you seriously begin to consider drinking again and/or committing suicide, force yourself to wait until the next day. What a difference a day makes!
- Seek medical treatment, even if you only suspect the presence of clinical depression. Be sure to tell your doctor that you are a recovering alcoholic. (Depression is now treatable. Remedies include medications, psychotherapy, interpersonal therapy, cognitive therapy, behavioral therapy and, rarely, electroconvulsive therapy. Each form of treatment can work in the appropriate situation. What won't work is alcohol "therapy.")
- Stick to your treatment. Give it time. It will work.
- Reward yourself for every little victory over depression and alcoholism. (See Appendix E.) (Actually, there are no "little" victories when dealing with these deadly diseases.)

SECTION V

MENTAL-EMOTIONAL TRAPS

Section V

MENTAL-EMOTIONAL TRAPS

"We have met the enemy and it is us."   Pogo

The most subtle and seductive relapse traps are the ones we set for ourselves. Emotional and mental traps are often more dangerous than physical ones. If mind games and emotions take over, recovery suddenly becomes a lot more fragile.

When alcoholics are emotionally overwrought (too happy, too sad, too angry, too scared, too jealous, etc.), it's easy to lose sight of sobriety. Emotions are chaotic. Sobriety requires structure and discipline.

Extreme emotions, unchecked, commonly cause people to . . .

- act unreasonably
- focus on instant gratification
- be short-sighted and unconcerned about consequences
- exercise poor judgment and make unhealthy choices
- be increasingly self-absorbed
- live for the moment and pull out all the stops
- become impatient and uninhibited.

Often, these reactions are more pronounced among alcoholics than in the general population. Obviously, these behaviors are not recovery-friendly. One of the first steps to sobriety is to achieve greater emotional stability.

Emotions are what make you human. They add passion to your life but uncontrolled, they can lead to trouble. Emotions that carry you to great heights or plunge you into great depths, make you especially vulnerable to self-destructive behaviors.

Relapse occurs when your emotions rule your life. Recovery occurs when you learn to moderate your emotions and temper feelings with reason and responsibility.

In a moment of emotion, it's easy to reverse a recovery that has been months in the making. Sound stupid? It is! Nevertheless, it happens every day. You can choose to keep it from happening to you.

This section identifies those volatile emotional states which are most likely to trigger a slip or a relapse and offers workable ways to keep these emotions in check to stay sober. They can work for you if you let them.

Trap #42 - Cravings

Some cravings are purely physical reactions to withdrawal. These are the easy ones. They will diminish with time. The most devious and dangerous cravings are emotional and psychological.

These won't go away by themselves. They can be obsessive and progressive. They can dominate your waking hours and creep into your dreams at night. They can make you crazy, especially during the early phases of recovery. Strong emotional and mental cravings will win out every time if you let them.

Emotional and psychological cravings can trigger

relapses because they wear down resistance. Many sober drunks, with the best of intentions, give in to cravings. Often they become preoccupied with romanticized thoughts about drinking and fooled by false memories of good times they *never* had. When this happens, the cravings blot out bad memories. Temptation begins to undermine self-confidence.

After a while, a sense of powerlessness over alcohol returns. Once you've convinced yourself that you can't hold out, you won't. Fortunately, cravings that are self-made can also be self-defeated.

Cravings are only as powerful as you allow them to be. The secret is to have a plan for dealing with them. You don't have to be superman or superwoman to withstand mind games, temptations and cravings. You just have to be super-prepared with strategies that will keep your thinking straight and your emotions in tow.

Don't con yourself into drinking again. The steps below can keep you *resistant* to cravings and *persistent* in your sobriety. Don't be misled by their simplicity–they work. Of course, they won't help unless you try them. Why not start today?

Action Plan

- Stay away from people and situations that may start you thinking ("stinking thinking") about booze. Avoid smoking and other behaviors associated with drinking.
- Realize that cravings will go away whether you drink or not.
- Plan in advance what you'll do when the craving

starts. Then, do it!

- Keep reminding yourself of your most important reasons for quitting drinking.
- "Play the whole tape." Allow yourself to recall all of the negative and demeaning consequences you've suffered because of alcohol.
- Keep busy. Take on new responsibilities at work, if you're ready. Don't allow time in your day for thinking about drinking.
- Volunteer to help at a detox center, work with an AA group for convicts or answer an AA hotline. (Twelfth Step work.) Witnessing others' misery is a vivid reminder of what you've been through. It can do a lot to chase away cravings.
- Read the literature on cravings and relapse. (See Appendix F.) Know what you're dealing with. There is power in understanding.
- Build up your resistance and self-confidence with positive self-talk. (See Appendix D.)
- When cravings start, take counteracting measures immediately. Call your counselor or sponsor. Recite the Serenity Prayer. Get to an AA meeting. Reread your "drinking history" or your 5th Step personal inventory.
- Distract yourself. Chew gum. Take a cold shower. Get physical. It's amazing how cravings fade during vigorous exercise.
- Practice relaxation techniques. Remove yourself psychologically. Mind games can work *for* you, as well as against you.
- Hold mental conversations with yourself. Talk yourself out of the craving.

- Do something that's more fun than drinking or thinking about drinking. (See Appendix C.)
- When the cravings are worst, pray your hardest.
- Reward yourself every time you outlast a craving. (See Appendix E.)

Trap #43 - Stress

Stress is the product of excess–too many demands, too many bosses, too many expectations, too many bills, too many problems, etc. Sobriety is the product of moderation. The two are mutually exclusive.

Successful and lasting recovery depends on eliminating excesses and reducing harmful stress. An important part of staying sober is finding ways to mellow-out without drinking.

Most drunks know a lot about stress but not much about how to eliminate it, handle it or use it constructively. They're accustomed to pouring stress relief out of a bottle. They don't have a clue about how to deal with problems and pressures when they're sober. That's one reason why relapse is still the norm among alcoholics.

Alcoholics need to find new tools and learn new skills for dealing with stress to stay sober. Treatment helps. Counseling can help. AA also helps. Much, however, has to be earned and learned on your own.

One of the first things to learn is–stress is a killer. It kills in many ways; alcoholism is just one of them. You have to be serious about managing and mastering stress if you're serious about sobriety.

Everyone could use a little stress relief but for recovering alcoholics, it's a matter of survival.

The action plan below contains proven stress reducers. Some of the suggestions are specifically designed for alcoholics. Use them to build your own coping plan. Do it for yourself! Do it now!

Action Plan

- Keep your priorities straight. First is God, second comes family, third, your sobriety, fourth is work, then everything else.
- Simplify your life–go back to the basics. Cut back and cut out. Focus on relationships, not possessions. Learn to say "No," and make it stick.
- Practice prayer and meditation. Don't just pray about "turning things over to your Higher Power," do it!
- Repeat the Serenity Prayer often enough to make it part of your life. It's the best single-source solution for negative stress.
- Persist in working the 12 Steps of AA. Each is a stepping stone toward serenity.
- Talk about your feelings, problems and stresses with your family, your sponsor and your AA group(s).
- Continue going to AA meetings. The mere act of attendance helps lower stress.
- Find a safe, personal retreat. Go there when you need to.
- Learn that less can be more. (Less controlling and less perfectionism can mean more serenity.)
- Recognize your limitations. Lower your expectations if you need to.

- Work on your religious life. Attend church and sing in the choir. Join a Bible study group. Spirituality is another name for peace.
- Stay away from people who anger, threaten, frustrate or intimidate you, including old drinking buddies.
- Get organized. Plan ahead, make lists and follow them.
- Practice relaxation techniques such as, yoga, deep breathing exercises and taking "mental vacations" on a daily basis.
- Cut down on caffeine, nicotine and sugar.
- Don't take tranquilizers unless prescribed by a physician who is familiar with your alcoholism.
- Get enough sleep and rest.
- When you feel stressed, ask, "Whose problem is it?" and "Which of the 12 Steps applies?" Let the answers guide your actions.
- Remember why you have to stay sober.
- Take to heart popular AA sayings (i.e., One day at a time, etc.). They're proven stress-busters.
- Hang around little children. It will help you remember what's really important.
- Listen to music. It really does soothe the savage breast.
- Gain as much control as you can over your job and your life.
- Build flex-time into your day. Schedule time for yourself.
- Get plenty of exercise. Everyone recommends it for reducing stress.
- Learn conflict resolution techniques, such as active listening, brainstorming solutions, reflecting,

rephrasing and negotiating.

- ► Break down big jobs into smaller, manageable tasks.
- ► Do something you really like for at least 30 minutes every day.

Trap #44 - Loneliness

Loneliness is one of the most terrifying and devastating emotions anyone can experience. It's not only physical separation from other human beings. There's a vast difference between being alone and feeling lonely.

Profound loneliness is a feeling of being completely and irrevocably cut off from all support, love, care and emotional contact with anyone, anywhere. It is closely associated with helplessness, depression and despair. (Only lonely people commit suicide.) Loneliness is a menacing, emotional relapse trap.

When an alcoholic feels totally alone in the universe and believes no one cares, it's easy to conclude there's no good reason to refrain from drinking. Of course, the truth is, there are always good reasons to stay sober. The trick is to identify them and to cling to them–no matter what.

Loneliness commonly occurs among drunks who have "hit bottom" and are starting to get sober. When drunks first stop drinking, it's natural to feel lonely. They are uncomfortable in an unfamiliar new world and no longer fit into their old one. Often, they have driven away old friends and supporters and have not yet replaced them with new ones. It can seem as if no one else has ever walked this path before and no one understands what they're going through.

Breaking down this sense of isolation is precisely why Alcoholics Anonymous was formed in the first place and why it works today. AA overcomes loneliness by linking people who know what it's like to drink and to be a drunk. AA members try to get better together.

ⵏLoneliness is usually self-imposed and self-perpetuating. Recovering alcoholics, feeling victimized, vulnerable and afraid, frequently create their own illusion of loneliness. (You're never as lonely as you think you are.) Fortunately, each person has the built-in capacity to conquer loneliness. It's part of being human.

You can take many steps to escape the loneliness trap, to reconnect with the real world and to form newer, richer relationships.

Tip: drinking isn't one of them. A substance that makes you sick, makes you smell bad and makes you act crazy, isn't going to solve your loneliness problem.

Try the measures below instead. You're only as lonely as you allow yourself to be!

Action Plan

▸ Use the AA advantage. If you live in a metropolitan area, meetings are held every hour of the day and night. Seek them out. You can always find companionship and more at an AA meeting.
▸ Reach out to others. Make the first move. Make new friends. Join. Volunteer. Take classes. If you're

lonely, it's not someone else's fault. It's yours!

- Pray. "Make conscious contact" with your God. You're never alone or lonely if you believe in a Higher Power.
- Make amends to those you've harmed. It's a way to rebuild old relationships.
- Enjoy humor. Laughter dispels loneliness.
- Consider getting a pet. An animal can be the best friend you'll ever have.
- Learn to enjoy your own company. Forgive yourself, accept yourself, and become your own best friend. It's even okay to talk to yourself.
- Awareness is a gift of sobriety. Use it to be alert and open to new experiences and possible connections.
- Compare your sober loneliness with what you experienced when you were drinking. Lying, cheating, sneaking and hiding create the worst kind of loneliness. You're better off sober.
- Read widely. You can lose a lot of loneliness in the pages of a good book.
- Use the phone, the internet and/or the postal service to reconnect with people you care about but who are far away.
- Provide your own validation through self-affirmations. (See Appendix D.)
- Perform community service to help other people. The more you get outside yourself, the less lonely you'll be.
- Remember. You're staying sober for yourself, not for anyone else. Recovery doesn't require company.
- If nothing else works, seek help from professionals who have been trained to deal with victims of

loneliness (i.e., psychologists, counselors, priests, etc.).

Trap #45 - Anger

Anger and alcohol often go together but they don't mix well. Anger is an ugly, self-punishing emotion that can get you in trouble, give you a heart attack or bring on a relapse.

In many ways, anger is an alcoholic's worst enemy. Angry people are out of control, they do crazy things.

- They can't think straight.
- They lose all objectivity.
- They act without thinking.
- Other people control their emotions and actions.

If all this sounds like a list of warning signs for a pending relapse, it is!

To make matters worse, anger is never a passive emotion, it demands acting out. Angry people have to do something–smash objects, fight, swear, drink– to release emotional energy. Anger is a trap sober drunks have to watch out for most.

Alcoholics often have lots of things to be angry about, but no one of them is worth risking relapse. Fortunately, help is available. Anger is a controllable emotion.

The best advice for recovering alcoholics is, don't get mad; don't get even; and don't get drunk! Do what many relapse counselors and anger-management experts recommend. Follow the action steps below.

Action Plan

- ▸ Remember the 3-A's for handling anger-provoking situations: **A**lter; **A**dapt; or **A**void. In other words, change the situation, adjust to it or walk away from it.
- ▸ Spend time with AA members. They're usually quite mellow people.
- ▸ Ask yourself, "Is my anger justified?" Don't rage over trifles.
- ▸ Change your way of thinking about people and things that provoke anger in you. Reframe the situation. Instead of thinking of irritating co-workers as annoyances, think of them as people to be pitied. How *you* construct your reality drives your emotional response.
- ▸ Rely on prayer to calm you down. The Serenity Prayer is great for putting anger in perspective. Turn more things over to a Higher Power.
- ▸ Let go of old grudges. Don't let ancient history jeopardize your present and future.
- ▸ Follow the classic Seven-Steps of Anger-Management:
  1. Understand what angers you.
  2. Know the symptoms of mounting anger.
  3. Know your tolerance levels.
  4. Avoid anger-producing situations
  5. Be assertively direct in addressing people and situations that upset you. Say what's on your mind, express what's bothering you, without anger.
  6. Do something physical and constructive to

dissipate anger (i.e., jog, garden, paint).
7. Act out anger in harmless ways (i.e., pound a pillow, write an angry letter and tear it up, etc.).
▸ Practice relaxation techniques before anger builds up.
▸ Learn conflict resolution skills for settling disputes peacefully. (Many community education programs now offer such training.)
▸ Watch how you say things, not just what you say.
▸ "When you're wrong, promptly admit it." (Step 10)
▸ When provoked, count to 10; then 20; then 100. Do whatever it takes to cool off before acting rashly.
▸ If necessary, seek professional counseling. It works.

Trap #46 - Guilt

"Guilt is a beast that never sleeps. Once you let it in and allow it to feed, it will only grow bigger and stronger until it consumes your life."
Mother's Wisdom (Contemporary Books, 1995)

All alcoholics feel guilty about something–some feel guilty about everything. Although all adults have guilt feelings, alcoholics seem especially susceptible to guilt feelings and guilt complexes. Some drunks can't get enough of guilt.

It's not surprising, then, that guilt is a major contributor to relapse. Guilt is a relentless and corrosive emotion. It eats away at self esteem until the "guilty party" begins to feel worthless or worse–the relapse trap is sprung.

When alcoholics initially get sober, they often

become fully aware of their own guilt and low self worth for the first time. It can be a devastating experience. This is what drives many recovering alcoholics back to the bottle. The cycle looks like this:

1. Guilt feelings.
2. Drinking to escape the guilt.
3. Increased guilt due to drinking.
4. Increased drinking (up the dosage) to escape increased guilt.
5. Repeat entire cycle.

Successful sobriety depends on breaking this cycle. AA is full of men and women who have done it. You can too.

Of course, no one can live entirely guilt-free. However, overcoming excessive guilt is possible. You can learn to live with normal guilt feelings without trying to drown or preserve them in alcohol. Here are the action steps that have helped many alcoholics to get past their guilt and move on with their recovery.

Action Plan

▸ Rework the 12-Steps of AA *with renewed effort*. Pay special attention to . . .

> Step 4 - Conduct a personal inventory.
> Step 5 - Admit past wrongs to God, yourself and another human being.
> Step 8 - List all you have harmed.
> Step 9 - Make direct amends.

▸ Ask forgiveness. Forgive others. Forgive yourself.
▸ Talk about your guilt feelings with your sponsor and

other recovering friends. It helps to know that others suffer from similar guilt. Uncorking bottled-up guilt often brings a sense of relief, cleansing and closure.

- Be open to second chances.
- Ask your Higher Power, "What is the right thing to do?" Act on the answer.
- Become honest and stay honest with other people. Live each day so you don't build up any additional guilt or shame.
- Accept responsibility for your past actions, but give due credit to alcohol as well.
- Realize that a relapse now will only add to your guilt.
- Give back to your community. Help others. You can't take back past mistakes but you can balance the scale with positive deeds in the present.
- Begin to rebuild your self-esteem with positive self-affirmations. (See Appendix D.) You are more than your guilt.
- Seek professional counseling or therapy if you're stuck in your guilt and are unable to move on with your life.

Trap #47 - Jealousy

Jealousy is an over-the-edge emotion. It is commonly linked with spousal abuse and other acts of domestic violence–including murder. The phrases "jealous rage" and "insanely jealous" are part of our everyday vocabulary. Obviously, jealousy is a volatile and dangerous state–jealousy coupled with alcohol can be a lethal combination.

Alcoholics are just as susceptible to jealousy as any other groups–maybe more so. Most alcoholics are extremely insecure; insecurity is a precondition for jealousy.

People can become jealous over almost anything (i.e., friends, lovers, jobs, possessions, etc.). Sometimes, recovering alcoholics even become jealous of old buddies because they are still drinking.

Jealousy makes people do things they wouldn't normally do. It can make fools of otherwise reasonable and intelligent individuals. Jealousy and relapse frequently go hand-in-hand.

Alcoholics who want to stay sober can't afford to be driven by jealousy. Sobriety requires clear-thinking, equanimity, discipline and acceptance. Jealousy involves just the opposite.

Don't let jealous emotions wreck your recovery. The "green-eyed monster" can be tamed. Let the action plan below show you how.

Action Plan

- Don't rush into any new relationships during the first year of recovery if you have a history of being possessive. Take your time. Don't allow jealousy to jeopardize your sobriety.
- Concentrate on communication in all of your relationships. Express feelings and concerns openly. Don't let suppressed emotions foment below the surface, only to erupt later in inappropriate or violent ways.

- Pray as much as you need to. The Serenity Prayer offers a formula for avoiding jealousy. Give control of outcomes to your Higher Power. It's not your job anyway.
- Use the AA slogans below to help create a calm mental attitude:
  Live and let live.
  One day at a time
  Easy does it
  Let go and let God.
  First things first.
  How important is it?
  Think!
- Make your feelings of jealousy a topic for discussion in your AA or treatment group. Let the group conscience help you find solutions.
- Remember, you are the *only* person you can change or control.
- Stay focused on your recovery. Jealously guard your sobriety–nothing else.
- Agree to call your sponsor and to wait one day before taking any jealous actions.
- Whenever you experience jealous feelings, write them down instead of acting them out. Then tear up what you've written.
- Don't confuse love and jealousy. True love is based on respect and trust. Jealousy is the product of fear, paranoia and mistrust.
- Relive in your mind the ugly things you've done out of jealousy. Did alcohol make things better? Or worse?
- Find and follow role models who understand how to

love and know how to be a friend. You probably have some in your AA group.

- ▸ Visit a battered woman's shelter and/or talk to victims of abuse. Seeing the results of uncontrolled jealousy is a powerful deterrent.
- ▸ Reward yourself whenever you avoid behaving jealously. (See Appendix E.)
- ▸ For additional suggestions, see Trap #45 (Anger).
- ▸ Seek professional counseling or therapy if you need it. It's never a sign of weakness to ask for help.

Trap #48 - Shame

Shame is defined as "A painful emotion caused by a strong sense of guilt, embarrassment, unworthiness, or disgrace." Sometimes called the "dismal emotion," shame ranks at the bottom of the emotional scale along with terror and depression. When it comes to relapse traps, it doesn't get much worse. Shame is a burden too heavy for some recovering alcoholics to bear.

People suffering from extreme shame feel utterly disgraced, dishonored and humiliated. (There's a difference between humility and humiliation.) Shame strikes at the very core of the human psyche–at what people think of themselves.

Like other emotions, shame is a learned response. People don't start to feel shame by themselves. Others convince them to feel that way. Our society is good at shaming people with problems and those of us with a drinking problem are definitely not exempt. Plenty of shaming of alcoholics is present in our culture.

Most alcoholics made many mistakes and have many regrets. They deserve to suffer the consequences of their actions but they don't deserve shame.

Becoming stuck in a permanent state of shame is a sure-fire way to guarantee a failed recovery. If you feel worthless, why not drink? What difference does it make? Who cares? Unabated shame can only lead to depression, hopelessness, despair, and perhaps, death by relapse.

Fortunately, it doesn't have to work that way. Redemption, amnesty and second chances are still possible. It starts with the amnesty you give yourself.

No one can make you feel shame unless you let them. Don't let them. Take positive actions to rise above shame, stay sober and rebuild a life you will be proud of. The only shame is in not trying. The time to start is now. Ready? Set. Go!

Action Plan

▸ Learn as much as you can about the disease concept of alcoholism. Becoming a drunk may be as much about a chemical imbalance as about character defects or moral weakness. Knowledge can take the sting out of shame.

▸ Make amends to those you've harmed–as much for you as it is for them.

▸ If you're Catholic, go to confession. If you're in AA, complete a fifth step (or repeat the step). Muster the courage to admit your faults to another human being. Do whatever it takes to get all of your wrongful acts out in the open. They never look as shameful in the light of day.

- Surround yourself with supportive, affirming people. That's what AA is all about.
- Pray. Meditate. Try to make contact with your Higher Power. Whatever you've done, God will forgive you. That's His job.
- Build on your strengths. Do what you do best and what you're most proud of to help re-establish self esteem and bury shame.
- Read inspirational literature, especially stories about reprieve, redemption, resurrection and renewal. Yours can be one of them.
- Take personal inventory. This time focus on your assets and the positive things in your life.
- Use positive self-talk--a lot! (See Appendix D.) Convince yourself you're okay–it's true.
- Make plans for the future. It's hard to feel shame when you're excited about something important yet to do.
- Adopt an attitude! Hold your head up high. Dare to be unashamed. It takes some moxie to be a recovering alcoholic these days. Don't just expect a miracle–act like one!
- Get involved in helping other alcoholics (12th Step work). Become a sponsor. Volunteer to be Trusted Servant for your AA group. When you help others realize they have nothing to be ashamed of, you help yourself in the process.

Trap #49 - Worry

"We are, perhaps, uniquely among the earth's creatures, the worrying animal."

Lewis Thomas

Alcoholics worry a lot. Insecurity, low self esteem, paranoid tendencies and a history of bad things happening to them may cause alcoholics to worry more than most folks. Sometimes, they worry themselves sick. Occasionally, they worry themselves into relapse.

Worrying is like inventing your own worst nightmare while you're still awake. Of course, most of the things alcoholics (and other people) worry about never happen. This makes it a non-productive activity and an empty emotion.

Worry, anxiety and doubt are not problem-solving techniques. In fact, they interfere with decision-making. Worse yet, they can have damaging physical effects. Worry contributes to high blood pressure, heart trouble, sleeplessness and, sometimes, relapse.

When alcoholics worry, they tend to blow things out of proportion, to dwell on worse case scenarios and to doubt their ability to persevere. Practicing alcoholics drink to chase away their worries and troubles. Recovering alcoholics worry about avoiding drinking to chase away their worries and doubts. Worrying doesn't help either group.

When worries mount up, drinking can seem like a plausible option again. Of course, it isn't. You know better. Protect yourself against relapse by learning to worry less and problem-solve more.

Use the strategies below to safe-proof your sobriety from excessive worry and self-doubt. You'll feel better, sleep better and have more fun. Don't worry, recovery is supposed to be like that.

Action Plan

▸ Revisit your favorite AA anti-worry slogans (i.e., One day at a time, Easy does It, Let go and let God, etc.). Repeat them often to integrate them into your reality.
▸ Read about worrying. Become a student of worrying. You'll soon find out most worries never come true.

> *"When I look back on all these worries, I remember the story of the old man who said on his deathbed that he had a lot of troubles in his life, most of which never happened."*
>
> Winston Churchill

The more you learn about worry, the less you'll have to worry about.
▸ Share your worries with trusted supporters, including family members and AA friends. They can help you sort out what's really worth worrying about.
▸ Remember the Serenity Prayer. It's all about how not to worry.
▸ Track your worries. List the things you worry about most. Monitor how many actually come true. Prove to yourself that worry isn't worth it.
▸ Don't worry at night, wait until morning. Things

never look so bleak in the daylight.

- Avoid whiners. Hang out with people who are upbeat and optimistic. AA is a good place to find them.
- Go back to church. Work on your spiritual life. If your faith is strong enough, you'll never have to worry again.
- Try to relax. Work out, take a bubble bath, have a massage. Tension and worry go together; reduce one and you reduce the other.
- Address your problems directly, don't just anguish over them. Make a plan for dealing with each of your worries. Taking action puts you back in control.

Trap #50 - Boredom

Many alcoholics are used to a live-action lifestyle full of crowds, noise, parties, music, bright lights and late hours. By contrast, recovery can seem insipid and BORING! Sometimes, recovering alcoholics are appalled by the prospect of a lifetime of sobriety and serenity. They can't imagine how they're going to fill their days and nights. What will they do for fun? What about excitement? It's common for newcomers to sobriety to question if they can make it over the long haul. Sobriety looks too quiet, too dull, too boring.

Fears about boredom loom larger in the mind than they play out in real life. Veteran AA members know that life can be richer, more rewarding and just as exciting when you're sober enough to know what's going on and to remember it afterwards. Nevertheless, boredom can be a legitimate threat to sobriety.

If "idle hands are the devil's tools," imagine how dangerous idle minds are. When people (including alcoholics) are bored, they become nervous, anxious, irritable and depressed. In this mental state, drinking with the old gang can sound good and a little slip doesn't seem so bad. Newcomers to sobriety need to guard against boredom. It's easier than you think.

Boredom is a flimsy excuse for relapse. You're only as bored as you allow yourself to be. It's entirely possible to live an exciting, thrill-packed, worthwhile life and be stone, cold sober also. Millions live that way every day. How do they do it? Check out the action plan below.

Action Plan

- Really focus on ONE DAY AT A TIME. A lifetime without booze may seem too dull and uneventful to deal with—one day you can handle.
- Try something new that you were always too drunk, too sick or too broke to do in the past. Take a class, travel, buy that book you've been dying to read. You could learn a foreign language or even try skydiving. Many more new things are out there to explore than you can fit into one sober lifetime.
- Find out about all of the non-alcoholic activities available in your community. Check Appendix C for ideas.
- Give the AA crowd a chance. Go where they go and do what they do. You'll probably have more fun than you think you will.
- Don't even think about going honky-tonkin' with the

old crowd and drinking only soda. It won't work during early recovery; it's too much pressure. Tempting fate is not a stay-sober technique.

- Challenge your body. Try new sports and/or work out at the gym or spa. Become too tired to be bored.
- Revisit some of your old interests, hobbies and pastimes.
- Learn to "chill out" without booze. Try a variety of relaxation techniques until you find what works best for you.
- Enjoy the contemplative life. Learn to think, plan, dream and wonder again.
- Explore the Internet. You will find enough there to keep you interested for years.
- Keep busy with work, volunteering, church activities, etc. Don't give yourself time to be bored.
- Fulfill obligations and commitments you've neglected for a long time. Spend time with your children. That's never boring.
- Be willing to put up with a little boredom. It beats getting sick, blacking out, being in an accident, having a fight or getting arrested. Dare to be bored once in awhile.

Trap #51 - Denial

Denial is an intrinsic part of the illness of alcoholism. It is what makes the disease so devious, deceptive and difficult to diagnose. Denial is a mind game alcoholics get good at playing. Unfortunately, it carries over into recovery.

Too many alcoholics practice denial even when they're sober.

- They deny they're scared.
- They deny they're thinking about drinking again
- They deny they have compelling cravings
- They deny they're lonely
- They deny they need more help.

When denial is present, the likelihood of relapse increases.

Denial is a problem-avoider, not a problem-solver. As long as you're in a state of denial, you can't work on your problems or get the support you need.

Successful sobriety requires rigorous honesty. Denial is lying to yourself and others. You have to overcome denial in order to safeguard your sobriety from relapse. It's not always easy to do.

Denial is a habit alcoholics *deny* having–it's second nature. Nevertheless, you can learn to quit denying just as you learned to quit drinking. Telling the truth can become a natural way of living but it usually takes some outside help.

The good news is–help is there when you need it and want it. Some of that help is found in the suggestions below.

Action Plan

► Find and keep a tough counselor or sponsor. You need one who can see through your pretenses and keep you honest. The best won't negotiate, look the other way or put up with foolishness. "Tough love" is what you need to help break the denial habit.

- Stick with the same AA group over time. The members will soon learn to spot when you're being phony and won't be bashful in telling you about it.
- Complete Step 5–Searching and fearless inventory–of the AA program. If you do it right, you've already left denial far behind.
- Pray for the strength to tell the truth–even to yourself.
- Ask family members and friends to give you feedback when they think you're distorting or ignoring reality.
- Listen to what you're telling yourself and others. Is it the truth? Learn to be your own watchdog.
- Try telling the truth 100% of the time for one day. Then, two days–and so on. It gets easier; it simplifies your life; it feels good; it *can* become a habit.
- Observe denial in others. (It's easy to spot if you know them well.) Is it helping them? Would they be better off admitting the truth? Apply the answers to your own life.
- Accept that it's okay to have problems. Everybody does. If it's okay to have them, it's okay to admit them, to talk about them and to face them without denial.
- Write down the denial phrases you used most frequently in the past such as. . . .
    I'm fine.
    Everything's great.
    Don't worry about me.
    Don't worry about it. I don't.
    I'm O.K. Just leave me alone
    It's no problem.

When you hear yourself repeating them and you feel yourself getting defensive, watch out! Stop, think, be honest.

- ► Keep a journal. Sometimes it's easier to write down the truth about how you feel and what's going on in your life than to say it out loud. Either way, you're beginning to be honest.
- ► Learn the physical signs of denial (lying) you exhibit. We all have some, such as rapid blinking, turning red, avoiding eye contact, or fidgeting. When you "see" yourself practicing denial, 'fess up' and tell the truth.
- ► Reward yourself every time you resist denial. (See Appendix E.)

Trap #52 - Insecurity (Lack of Confidence, Low Self Esteem)

"No one can make you feel inferior without your consent." Eleanor Roosevelt

Most drunks are insecure. Despite a facade of bravado and flamboyant behavior, self-doubt frequently drives alcoholics. In fact, insecurity, lack of self-confidence and low self esteem are primary reasons many alcoholics start drinking in the first place. They're also the reasons why many would-be recovering alcoholics repeatedly slip back into relapse. Until an alcoholic regains a positive sense of self worth, relapse is inevitable.

You're never going to succeed at sobriety until you

become convinced you are capable and worthwhile. How you see yourself determines how you handle recovery.

One of the biggest differences between winners and losers in any endeavor is that winners believe in themselves. The same difference separates those who continually struggle with their sobriety and those who confidently maintain long-term, uninterrupted recovery.

Liking yourself and having a positive self image are essential to survival and sobriety. Until you achieve an "I can" attitude, you can't!

Insecurity is a learned emotion. Fortunately, it can be unlearned. Many people are willing and ready to put you down. However, they can't make you feel inferior or insecure unless you let them.

You won't find confidence in a bottle but you can find it through positive thoughts and actions. Pride and self-confidence can be self-taught. Many ways are available for you to enhance your self image and increase the odds in favor of successful recovery. Some of the best ones are listed below.

Choose the actions that suit your needs and write your own coping plan. You'll be glad you did. It will make you feel good about yourself again. Who deserves it more?

Action Plan

▸ Learn more about the disease concept of alcoholism. The more you understand the nature of the illness, the better you'll feel about yourself. You're sick, not worthless.

- Assess your strengths. Start with awareness of the support and love you already have in your life. Recall your past successes. Review your accomplishments over the past 12 months. Count your blessings; you'll find you're better off than you thought.
- Associate with people who believe in you. Stick close to family. You can also count on AA members for support and unconditional love.
- Give yourself positive internal messages (self affirmations). See Appendix D.
- Set reasonable expectations. Be satisfied with progress. Don't demand perfection for yourself.
- Work on improving yourself. Take assertiveness classes or martial arts training. They'll give you confidence, as well as new skills.
- Look your best. Pay attention to grooming. Try a new hairstyle. Dress for success. If you look good, you'll feel good about yourself. A make-over can do wonders for self esteem.
- Take care of your physical needs (nutrition, exercise and rest). The better you feel, the better you feel about yourself.
- Try new things. Risk-taking is a great confidence-booster.
- Read inspirational literature (i.e., *Chicken Soup for the Soul*, Canfield and Hanson) and listen to recovery tapes. Take their optimistic messages to heart. Dare to hope.
- Get your quota of hugs. Plenty are available at most AA meetings.
- Focus on your distinctiveness. What is it that you

know more about or do better than most people? Find ways to showcase your talents.

- ▸ Make plans. Find a purpose. Have something worthwhile yet to do. Having important unfinished business is a powerful morale booster.
- ▸ Celebrate your successes, great or small.
- ▸ Volunteer to help homeless alcoholics. Helping others always makes you feel good inside. It's hard to be down on yourself when you see others who are worse off.
- ▸ For other ideas, see suggestions for Traps #41 (clinical depression), #48 (shame) and #49 (worry).
- ▸ If nothing else works, seek professional counseling or therapy. Don't give up. God doesn't make throwaway people.

Trap #53 - Happiness (Celebration of good fortune)

Can there be a downside to happiness and good fortune? You bet. Happiness is a good thing. How people handle it can be devastating and self-destructive.

When alcoholics, or anyone else, experience good fortune (i.e., getting a promotion, inheriting some money, winning the lottery, being recognized with an award, etc.), it's easy to get carried away. Good fortune is heady stuff. It not only generates happiness, it produces a rush of euphoria, a sense of power and an expansive feeling of invincibility. This isn't necessarily a good thing for recovering alcoholics.

The first response to good fortune for most people is

to celebrate. Let's party! Champagne often comes to mind. When you're high on happiness, success or good luck, it's only natural to want to throw caution to the wind. This is a bad plan if you're trying to stay sober.

Some recovering alcoholics can't stand prosperity. When they realize some good fortune, they blow it by overreacting. Don't be one of them. Don't let your good times turn bad.

Relish your happiness and good fortune–you deserve it–but don't let it trap you into thinking you can get away with cheating a little on your sobriety. Happiness is not a good reason to relapse.

You can learn to handle happiness and celebrate good fortune without drinking or risking relapse. Use the following ideas for starters. Enjoy!

Action Plan

▸ When good fortune strikes, find non-alcoholic ways to celebrate, have fun and pamper yourself. (See Appendices C and E.)

▸ If your good fortune calls for a party, check the cautions and suggestions for Trap #22 (Party Time).

▸ Share your happiness and celebrate with sober friends.

▸ Don't do anything your sponsor (or your mother) wouldn't approve of. Ask your sponsor and AA friends to pull you up short if you start to get cocky or go overboard.

▸ Remember past celebrations that got out of hand when you were drinking. Don't make the same mistake again.

- Talk to your AA group members about how they handle happiness. You don't have a monopoly on good ideas.
- Pray for "good sense" when you're feeling on top of the world. You don't want to fall off.
- Remember that good fortune can be short-lived. Relapse can be permanent.
- No matter how much success, happiness or good luck you experience, value your humility. You're still "powerless over alcohol."

Trap #54 - Good Memories (Euphoric Recall)

Recovery is hard. If it wasn't, everybody would do it. Nobody ever said that getting and staying sober would be easy. The early stages of recovery are particularly marred by painful physical reactions to withdrawal, powerful cravings, guilt feelings and an epidemic of doubts and fears. During this stage many recovering alcoholics revert to euphoric memories of their former drinking life.

It's natural for the mind to blot out bad memories and preserve only the good ones. Many alcoholics, struggling with sobriety, become easily distracted by false memories of what it was like when they were drinking. Life seemed carefree and every day was a party. Of course, what they remember and what truly happened may be worlds apart.

The trouble with euphoric recall is it makes things seem better than they were. What you recall is a life that never was. It's fun to remember the good times but it's even more important to remember the blackouts, the hangovers, the DUI arrests and all the other painful consequences of abusing alcohol.

When things get rough in recovery, it's tempting to accept your mind's romanticized version of what life was like before you stopped drinking. Don't. It's a mind trap. It can, and often does, lead to a relapse. Don't be fooled by your own selective memory. It's better to accurately recall unpleasant events than to relive them all again following a relapse.

When euphoric memories begin to take over, it's time for a wake-up call. Give yourself a reality check. Use the steps below to get real and stay sober. Remember it like it really was and you won't ever want to go back to drinking again!

Action Plan

- ▸ "Play the whole tape." Force yourself to remember the bad times, as well as the good.
- ▸ Focus on the good things which are happening since you got sober–they're real. Many of your memories are only fantasy.
- ▸ Reread the history of your story with alcohol that you prepared in treatment. It will remind you it wasn't all fun and games.
- ▸ Complete Step 4 of the AA program–Make a searching and fearless moral inventory. Review all of the consequences you've suffered. Were the "good" times worth it?
- ▸ Stay away from old haunts and old drinking cronies while you're bothered by euphoric memories.

- Listen to the stories other alcoholics have to tell. How much fun were they having when they hit bottom?
- Remember what you looked like and felt like when you first stopped drinking or entered treatment.
- When you're making amends to those you've harmed, ask them if you were having a good time while you were drinking.
- Stay in frequent contact with your sponsor and other AA members whenever you're tempted by euphoric memories. Ask them to help keep you out of trouble. If necessary, go to more AA meetings than usual until the state of euphoric recall passes.
- Visit a detox center. It's like looking in a mirror at your old self. *Nothing* is euphoric about the experience.
- Pray for persistence and resistance to see you through any period of euphoric memories.
- Get involved in Mothers Against Drunk Driving (M.A.D.D.). Talking to persons who have lost loved ones due to alcohol-related accidents or manslaughter quickly removes the glamour from drinking and replaces romanticized memories with grisly reality.
- No matter how intense the euphoric memories get, always put off drinking for one day. That's all it usually takes to return you to reality.
- Remember that euphoric memories, like cravings, will fade whether you drink or not.

Trap #55 - Bad Memories (Painful recall)

As explained previously, good memories (euphoric recall) can set the stage for relapse. Bad memories (painful recall) can do the same thing. In fact, painful memories are often greater facilitators of relapse than good ones.

For many alcoholics, the beginning phase of recovery is the first time they've ever become fully aware of their past actions or had to face head-on what a mess they've made of their lives. It is often a devastating and traumatic experience.

Sobriety can open up Pandora's box of humiliation, guilt and shame. Sometimes it is overwhelming for many alcoholics to finally become accountable for years of mayhem and misconduct. Memories of missed opportunities, broken promises, ruined relationships, lost loves, abusive behavior, money problems and brushes with the law are almost too much for some to bear.

To make matters worse, memory frequently distorts reality, making past mistakes seem more disastrous than they really were. When confronted with memories seemingly too painful to deal with, some alcoholics seek the only relief they've ever known–booze! It doesn't work. Relapse doesn't eliminate painful recall, it makes it worse.

There are better ways to put painful memories into perspective and use them as the basis for building a new life. Let the ideas below show you how to lay bad memories to rest without anesthetizing them with alcohol.

Don't forget your past mistakes but don't allow the

memory of them to immobilize you either. Follow a middle road using the markers that follow.

Action Plan

▸ Use the suggestions for Traps #46 (Guilt), #48 (Shame) and #56 (Insecurity). These strategies will work for painful recall as well.

▸ Make amends. It's the best you can do to right past wrongs. No one can expect more.

▸ Attend a variety of AA meetings and listen to the stories of other alcoholics. Many have done worse things than you and are now sober and successful.

▸ Ask trusted, long time acquaintances about your past mistakes and misbehavior. You may find out they weren't as awful as you remember.

▸ Notice how quickly most people forgive and forget. How many celebrities can you name who have committed worse discretions than yours and still receive public acclaim and acceptance. It can happen to you, too.

▸ Repeat the Serenity Prayer every day–twice! It holds the secret for making peace with your painful memories.

▸ Talk about your guilt and your remorse. People will believe you. Now you just have to learn to believe yourself.

▸ Keep busy. Make plans for the future. Get excited about where you're going, instead of dwelling on where you've been.

▸ Keep track of all the successful people in your community who are recovering alcoholics. You're in good company. They all made mistakes. If they can bounce back, you can too!

▸ Remember, you didn't screw up all by yourself, alcohol was a big part of the equation. Be sure to factor alcohol out of your life from now on.

▸ Use the story of your errors and excesses to help keep others from making similar mistakes.

Trap #56 - Loss of Spirituality

Most alcoholics purposely distance themselves from their church, their religion and their God. They don't pray, they don't read scriptures, and they don't worry much about their soul. The spirits in their life take precedence over their spiritual life. As may be expected, this loss of spirituality can spell disaster for them during recovery.

Without some faith in a power greater than self, relapse is likely–perhaps inevitable. Alcoholics Anonymous and most other responsible alcohol treatment and rehabilitation programs rely on some form of spirituality to assist recovery. If this cornerstone is left out, the programs seldom work.

A drunk, who has already proved to be "powerless over alcohol," doesn't have much chance of getting and staying sober all alone. It takes something stronger than individual will and determination. Nobody escapes alcoholism without help.

Spirituality is indispensable to sobriety. Specific, formal religious belief or denominational affiliation is not essential to boost recovery, but it does take faith in some Higher Power. For some alcoholics, this Higher Power may only be an AA group. Their faith and trust can only stretch that far at the time. Through experience and spiritual growth, however, they may redefine their personal Higher Power as time goes by.

Reconnect with your spiritual life if you're serious about sobriety. You can restore Faith and prayer can work again, but it won't happen by accident.

Tap the resources of your Higher Power. You know you need the help. You have nothing to lose but a deadly disease. You gain everything! If you don't know where to start, try the simple action steps below. Godspeed!

Action Plan

- ▸ Try prayer again. If it seems awkward at first, it will get better and easier with practice. Start by repeating the Lord's Prayer and the Serenity Prayer. You can improvise later.
- ▸ Be conscientious about working on the 12-Steps of AA. Even if you don't believe in everything they believe in, do it anyway. Start by going through the motions and you may end up living that way.
- ▸ Go to church or synagogue. The first step to spirituality is to show up—often!
- ▸ Read inspirational and spiritual literature. Start with the Big Book of AA and move up to the Bible or Torah when you are ready.
- ▸ Behave as if you're religious (even if you're not). Follow the Golden Rule and the Ten Commandments. Help others. It can become a habit.
- ▸ Talk to your sponsor and AA group about their

beliefs and spirituality. Faith has been known to be contagious.

- Visit a newborn nursery. Volunteer in an elementary school. It's hard not to believe in miracles and a Higher Power when you're around little children.
- Give both God and yourself a second chance.
- Talk to a minister, priest or rabbi about your doubts and fears. They're not as judgmental as you may think. You'll probably be surprised by how much help you get.
- Make the spiritual dimension as important in your new life as a bottle was in your old one. It's a life-saving trade off.
- Ask others to pray for you. It's another way friends can help.
- Hang out with believers. Observe how they live their faith. Does it seem worth it?
- If nothing else works, try a new church or denomination. It may be what you need to jump start your spiritual life.
- Do something extra to reach out to your Higher Power. Sing in the choir. Volunteer to be an usher at church. Attend prayer breakfasts. Join a Bible Study group. Give it your best shot. You won't regret it.
- Find a quiet time and place to be alone. Go there often. (*"God is a friend of silence."* - Mother Teresa)

SECTION VI

ATTITUDE TRAPS

Section VI

ATTITUDE TRAPS

In many ways, you are your attitudes. The biases, point of view, state of mind, disposition or persona you adopt defines your world and how you act in it.

Attitudes are filters through which we screen our perceptions of reality. If we alter our attitude, we change our world.

It's no surprise, then, that attitudes sometimes get us into trouble. Unfortunately, alcoholics are notorious for both bad attitudes and getting into trouble. They can even carry over into recovery.

Sobriety is based on honesty, not posturing. False bravado or phony attitudes can jeopardize it. You know alcoholics whose attitudes get in the way of their adjustment to sober living and keep them from getting the help they need. It's ironic when attitudes become relapse traps sabotaging sobriety but it happens every day.

The good thing about attitudes is you can change them. This section addresses the attitudes that frequently cause sobriety to slip away and common-sense pointers on how to change them before it's too late. Many approaches to attitude adjustment are available. This section contains some of the best. Help yourself.

Trap #57 - False Pride

"Pride goeth before destruction . . ."
Bible: Proverbs 16:18

The Biblical author of this proverb could have been writing about recovering alcoholics. False pride plays a key role in more relapses than any other self-defeating attitude.

Drunks who get sober and stay sober, have cause for justified pride. They've taken a risk. They've accomplished something many people can't pull off. Quitting drinking and staying dry takes guts, grit, commitment, discipline and perseverance. It's okay to be proud of it.

The problem occurs when alcoholics take their pride too far. They become deluded into thinking they did it all by themselves. Of course, it didn't happen that way. No one achieves sobriety without help.

Humility and gratitude are linchpins of long-lasting recovery. False pride denies both. Once an alcoholic takes full credit for his or her sobriety, he or she is well on the way to losing it.

Too many alcoholics get cocky after a few weeks or months of sobriety. They begin to think they can handle anything–including cheating on their sobriety. They may even start to believe they can control their drinking. Whoa! Exaggerated, "false" pride is a dangerous attitude for anyone who is admittedly "powerless over alcohol."

If you're going to succeed at sobriety, you have to leave false pride behind. It doesn't come naturally. You have to learn how to do it. Here are some learning aids that work. Don't be too proud to accept the help.

Action Plan

- Get a tough sponsor, someone who is brutally frank and honest–that's what sponsors are for. If your current sponsor lets you get away with false pride, look for a second sponsor who will tell it like it is.
- Make a Gratitude List of all those who have helped your recovery. Be honest. Your list may include family, friends, counselors, sponsors, AA members, clergy, doctors, police, lawyers, judges, co-workers or employers and don't forget your Higher Power. If there's no one on your list, you're lying!
- Read the literature on relapse. (See Appendix F.) What does it say about false pride?
- Stick with the 12-Steps of AA. You don't outgrow them. Pay special attention to Step 1 (powerlessness over alcohol) and Step 10 (continue to take personal inventory). Where does it say in the 12 Steps that you can start drinking again–even a little bit? Do the steps right; get rid of false pride.
- Talk to your AA group about your new-found feelings of pride and super-confidence. Is this a common attitude? Have others had it? What happened to them?
- Talk to patients in treatment for relapse. How did they get there? Did false pride play a role in their fall?
- Pray for humility and gratitude. You'll like the feeling.
- List all the benefits of sober living. Which ones are

you willing to give up in case you're wrong and you can't control your drinking?

- ► Learn all you can about the disease concept of alcoholism. No permanent cure exists; no such thing as controlled drinking is possible for an addict. Deal with it!
- ► Remember when you used to say:
  "I can handle it."
  "I'll just have a few."
  "I never get drunk."
  "I don't have a drinking problem."
  "I can quit any time."
  False pride was talking. How's that different from what you're thinking and saying to yourself now? Don't let history repeat itself.
- ► Remember your worst day when you were drinking? Is it worth the risk of feeling that way all over again just to gamble on your false pride?

Trap #58 - Complacency

Most self-destructive attitudes that trigger relapses occur early in recovery. Complacency is different. It can come out of nowhere at any time during the recovery period–even after years of sobriety.

Complacency is an underhanded attitude that lulls unsuspecting alcoholics into letting their guard down. After a long period of successful sobriety, it's easy to start taking things for granted. When everything is going smoothly, alcoholics often feel they don't have to try so hard anymore. Wrong!

Recovery is forever. It requires continuous vigilance–for life! No safe time when recovering alcoholics can let their defenses down exists. Just when they begin to assume everything is going to continue to be all right (without effort on their part), things can go all wrong in a hurry.

Don't let a false sense of security trick you into making a stupid (maybe lethal) mistake. Relapses can occur after five, ten or twenty years of sobriety. Complacency is frequently the cause.

Working hard at staying sober is natural when it's an exciting new experience. Later, over the long haul, it becomes more difficult to stay focused. However, staying focused is what it takes to continue sobriety.

Don't let a complacent attitude rob you of your sobriety. Keep your recovery fresh every day. The ideas below can make it easier.

Action Plan

- Continue doing what's worked so far–reading, working the 12-Steps and (important!) going to meetings. (The first sign of complacency is laxity in AA attendance.)
- If you feel that your recovery is getting stale, try a new AA group. The change may recharge your recovery batteries.
- Work with beginning AA members. Hearing their stories and witnessing their progress brings it all back to you and helps you stay engaged.
- Ask family members and your sponsor to let you know in no uncertain terms if you start to get sloppy

about your recovery.

- Attend speaker meetings and AA roundups that feature inspirational presenters. They never fail to give your recovery a boost.
- Become involved with activist organizations such as M.A.D.D. (Mothers Against Drunk Driving) and S.A.D.D. (Students Against Drunk Driving). The energy is contagious.
- Keep handy reminders of your alcoholism where you can't ignore them. Carry an AA medallion; keep AA literature in sight; use bumper stickers, T-shirts, and coffee mugs with AA messages. Don't allow yourself to forget where you came from.
- Share your experiences with others frequently. It's a way to help alcoholics still suffering and help yourself also.
- Try a retreat. It's a booster shot for an ailing recovery. Many treatment facilities now offer overnight or weekend retreats featuring lectures, counseling, group sessions, meditation and more.

Trap #59 - "I Owe it to Myself."

Some alcoholics operate on the erroneous notion they're doing the world a favor by getting sober. They do it to please or satisfy their family, their spouse or their boss. Unfortunately, they've stopped drinking for the wrong reasons. They should be doing it for themselves; not for others. The world doesn't care whether they're drunk or sober.

These so-called "dry drunks" may stay sober for a

while, but they're often unhappy and resentful because they cling to old perceptions, patterns and behaviors. They don't change their lives; they only change their drinking habits. It's not enough and it doesn't work.

Recovering alcoholics who think they're helping everyone but themselves eventually begin to feel they should be rewarded for their sacrifices. Frequently, they develop an "I owe it to myself" attitude. What they really think is:

- I've been good long enough.
- I'm due for some relief.
- I should get to do what I want to do for a change.
- I deserve a drink!

Obviously, this is a dead-end attitude that can lead nowhere except to the brink of relapse. Unless this train of thought is turned around, relapse will happem.

You and your recovery are in trouble if you have an "I owe it to myself" attitude. A radical attitude adjustment is called for. You need to take some giant steps and you need to take them now. Here they are–use them if you're serious about your sobriety.

Action Plan

▸ Consider repeating treatment or getting into an aftercare program. You've missed the point somewhere along the way.

▸ Rework the 12 Steps of AA. Be honest, be thorough. Try harder this time. If you do it right, you may save your life.

▸ Spend more time with your sponsor. (Think of your sponsor as a personal trainer for your recovery.)

- Have long talks about recovery. Discuss what it is, what it isn't, and why. Your sponsor may be the only one who can get your thinking back on track.
- Double-up on AA meetings. Saturate yourself with AA contacts. The more exposure you have, the more likely you may be to accept the AA program of recovery.
- Form your own recovery "think tank." Gather veteran recovering alcoholics whom you trust and respect. Discuss humility, gratitude and the meaning of recovery. If they can't help you change your thinking, who can?
- Read all you can about sobriety and recovery. Knowledge and understanding can help you make a mid-course correction.
- Talk to recovering alcoholics who have become successful members of your community. What was their motivation? How did they do it? How do they keep it up?
- Reevaluate your priorities. Consider these points:
  1. You don't need any other reward for staying sober. Sobriety is *the* reward.
  2. Your drunkenness may hurt others but you're the only one who is sure to die of it. Think about it!
- Change sponsors, switch AA groups, find a new counselor–do *something* to shake up your program and revitalize your recovery. The change may help change your attitude as well.

Trap #60 - "A Little Can't Hurt."

Alcoholics are good at fooling people. They're best at fooling themselves. At some point in recovery, many fool themselves into thinking "a little can't hurt." They're wrong. A little can hurt. Ask all the people in treatment after relapsing.

Every relapse starts with just "a little." Only one drink is still the first drink. Since when could you stop after the first drink?

Recovering alcoholics serious about sobriety, practice strict abstinence. Many even shy away from cough medicine or mouthwash containing alcohol. Why take chances?

Believing "a little can't hurt" is a red flag attitude. Practice caution whenever it starts to creep into your thoughts. Don't fool yourself.

A little drink can hurt. It happens hundreds of times every day. Alcohol is poison. Even a little can be lethal.

Positive thoughts and actions can change attitudes. Try the following to change your attitude and save your recover.

Action Plan

▸ Remember the last time you tried to stop drinking. Did you–could you–stop after just "a little?"
▸ Review Step 1 of the AA program. What does "powerless over alcohol" really mean?
▸ Read available literature about relapses. (See Appendix F.) Where does it say "A little can't hurt?"
▸ Let your sponsor talk you out of it.

155

- Ask ten AA friends if it's O.K. to drink "a little." If even one of them says "Yes," then go ahead. Too bad. It's unanimous. The "nays" have it.
- Check the action plan for Trap #42 (Cravings). The same steps will work for this attitude trap as well.
- Talk to people you know who have had one or more relapses. What was their downfall? Learn from their mistakes.
- Tell your AA group members how you feel. They know from experience why it won't work.
+ Ask yourself, "Even if a little can't hurt, what can it help?" Forget it!
- Focus on why you quit drinking. Don't take a chance–not even a "little" chance–of losing all you've gained.
- Remember the old AA axiom: "One drink is too many; ten aren't enough."
- If you decide to drink just "a little," wait one day. It's likely you'll change your mind by then.

Trap #61 - "What the Hell."

When you were drinking, life was spontaneous, spur of the moment, unpredictable and out-of-control. Much of what you did was showing off (false bravado). You didn't worry about consequences. You lived for the moment. What the hell!

Sobriety isn't like that. It's just the opposite. Recovering alcoholics may get tired of being disciplined, responsible and predictable. They get fed up with meditations, meetings and making amends. They yearn for more carefree days. They wish they could just say, "What the hell!" They can't—ever.

"What the hell" is an attitude trap. Lasting sobriety is based on remembering consequences, not ignoring them. Living for the moment is flirting with relapse, a flirtation that can wreck your recovery.

Adopting a "what the hell" attitude means you don't give a damn—but you do! You can beat this attitude by using the advice below.

Action Plan

▸ Pause to reflect how well off you are. Sobriety has been good to you. Don't do anything impulsive that might take it all away.

▸ Observe how drunks behave at parties and in other social or public situations. It's not a pretty sight.

▸ What can a "What the hell" attitude get you? Watch newcomers to AA. Observe their pain. Do you want to go through that again?

▸ Stay away from old haunts and old cronies whenever you're in a "What the hell" mood. Spend time with AA friends instead. Notice that those who are solid in their sobriety are no longer tempted to live only for the moment.

▸ Get reacquainted with the consequences of drinking and a "What the hell" attitude.
   √ Visit a detox center or a battered women's shelter.
   √ Ride with your local police on domestic abuse or traffic accident calls.
   √ Attend a candlelight vigil for victims of drunk

drivers.

If these experiences don't keep you sober, nothing will.

- Listen to the stories other alcoholics have to tell. It's like a broken record of highs and lows and lows and lows. Who needs it?

- Tell and retell your own story. Keep it fresh in your mind to help you remember what a "What the hell" attitude has done to your life.

- Re-do Step 4 of the AA program (taking personal inventory). Ignoring present and future consequences is hard when you review the pain you've suffered in the past.

- Talk to diabetic friends about how they cope with the need to be focused and disciplined every day. Diabetics and alcoholics have some things in common.

- Ask your Higher Power to "remove your shortcomings"–including your "What the hell" attitude.

- Ask your family and friends to tell you what you were really like in your "What the hell" days. If it sounds like a stranger, it is. You're a different person now–part of the miracle of recovery.

- Enjoy the serenity of your new life. It's the payoff for sobriety. You can't get it with a "What the hell" attitude.

- Pamper and reward yourself for staying sober and beating the "What the hell" attitude. (See Appendix E.)

Trap #62 - "I'm Cured."

After years of successful sobriety, it's hard for some alcoholics not to think of themselves as "cured." Despite medical and scientific evidence and AA experience to the contrary, they can't help thinking (hoping) maybe–just maybe—they've gotten over their alcoholism. Surely, they've recovered by now.

Wishful thinking is a universal human trait, pronounced among alcoholics, but wishing won't make it true.

If you believe you're cured, you're sicker than you think–and close to a relapse. The "I'm cured" attitude has seduced many long-term, sober alcoholics into relapse. It's one of the mind's cruel hoaxes, but it's worked on many well-intentioned, recovering alcoholics. Don't be one of them.

There is no permanent, fool-proof cure for alcoholism. It's not like acne, you won't outgrow it. Recovery is forever. The disease may hide but it never goes away. If you want to stay sober, you have to accept that fact and deal with it.

Don't fall for the "I'm cured" attitude trap. You're not and won't be cured but you don't have to be cured to stay away from booze–you only have to be diligent.

Let the strategies below remind you that you may not be cured, but you can stay sober anyway.

Action Plan

Become familiar with the medical facts about alcoholism–your counselor can help. Where does it say there's a cure?

- Re-do Step 1 of the AA program. Admit you're "powerless over alcohol." It doesn't mean you are powerless just for a while.
- Find another alcoholic who is "cured" to compare notes with. If you can't find one…hmmm. Think about it!
- Even if you think you're cured, you don't have to start drinking again to prove it. Just keep on doing what you've been doing. It's worked so far.
- Test your notion that you're cured on your sponsor and other AA members. If no one agrees with you, what does that tell you?
- Despite your "I'm cured" attitude, don't try drinking if your family and friends oppose it. You still owe them for overlooking your past transgressions and for sticking with you this far. It's part of making amends.
- Focus on Step 10 of the AA program. Continue to take personal inventory and when you are *wrong,* promptly *admit it.*
- Try again to follow Step 11 of AA as well. Pray only for "knowledge of *His* will and the power to carry it out."
- Try a buddy system. Arrange for a family or AA member to stick close by as long as you're wrestling with the cured/not cured issue. It's not only Pinocchio who needs a second party conscience. Recruit your own Jimminy Cricket to help keep you on track.
- Listen to your doubts.
- Go outside yourself. Concentrate on helping alcoholics with less sobriety than you(Twelfth Step

work). When you become involved and concerned with their progress, you won't be so hung-up on your own status.

▸ Watch what happens when other alcoholics take chances with their sobriety. Is it worth it?

Trap #63 - "I Don't Care."

Lasting recovery depends on "caring." You remain sober as long as you care about yourself, your family, your friends, your work and your life. Stop caring and recovery can unravel in a hurry.

Some alcoholics reach a point where they are tempted to succumb to an attitude of "I don't care." It usually happens when problems are piling up with no relief in sight. At such times, it's easy to think, "I've tried and I've tried and it's still too hard. I don't care any more."

Of course, no one ever said that sobriety would solve all your problems. It won't, but it may equip you to deal with them without killing yourself by drinking. If you quit caring completely, however, nothing will prevent you from relapsing. That's the trap.

Fortunately, the "I don't care" attitude is only temporary; because underneath you truly do care. You only need to be reminded. Caring can be rekindled!

Don't ever convince yourself you don't care. Stand up to the attitude–it's a phony. It won't survive the scrutiny of realistic thinking. Use the suggestions below to help recapture a caring attitude, so you can go on with your sobriety.

Action Plan

▸ Think about the people and things in your life that are worthwhile. Write them down. Wow! What a lot to care about.

▸ Take a day off and do those things you enjoy most. (See Appendices C & D.) It's hard not to care when you're having fun.

▸ Before you decide you don't care, ask yourself, "What happens to others?" Your co-workers? Your boss? Your spouse? Your children? Grandchildren? Maybe you do care after all!

▸ Start reciting the Serenity Prayer regularly. It works best when problems seem most insurmountable.

▸ Don't forget about the Lord's Prayer, either. It's a reminder that your Higher Power still cares about you.

▸ Return to a one-day-at-a-time life style. Difficulties become more manageable and it allows you to keep caring at the same time.

▸ Accept the love, respect and affection others offer you. Look for it. Your family shows it; your AA friends show it. They can't all be wrong–you are worth caring about.

▸ Use self-affirmations (See Appendix D.) to remind yourself you're worthwhile.

▸ Plan your future. Make exciting new goals. Hope and optimism easily drive out an "I don't care" attitude.

▸ Help others. Volunteer and support your favorite charity. If you care about others, you surely can care about yourself.

▸ Review your life's story. No matter how bad things

look now, they were worse when you were drinking. You've made progress.

- ‣ Read all the inspirational literature you can find. They're called "self-help" books for a reason. They can help you care again.
- ‣ Enjoy beauty by revisiting nature and reading poetry. They help make life worth caring about.
- ‣ Keep going to meetings. Something about an AA meeting buoys your spirits and makes you feel better about yourself.
- ‣ If you begin thinking you don't care anymore, don't give up too easily. Remember, drinking won't make your problems go away, it will only make you feel worse about yourself. Continue to show up and do what you're supposed to do. The negative attitude will pass. Time is on the side of caring.

Trap #64 - "Why Me?"

Americans love to be victims. Alcoholics are better at it than most. Victimization is a popular excuse today for lots of problem behavior–including relapse. Thinking as a victim, alcoholics get bogged down asking, "Why me?" It's easier to complain about being unfairly treated and singled out for suffering than it is to do something about their alcoholism.

Alcoholics who acquire a "Why me?" attitude are often looking for sympathy– and a reason to drink again. "Why me?" is a form of self-pity.

Tip: If it sounds like whining, it is whining.

Distracting yourself from sobriety by taking a "Why me?" attitude is entirely possible, but it won't work on others. Not many people want to attend your "pity party." It's your problem and you must deal with it. Others can *help* you stay sober but they cannot and will not do it for you.

Why you? It might be random selection; it might be genetic; it might be environmental. It doesn't matter! The important facts are that you are alcoholic but you can live without drinking–and without whining. The choice is yours.

If you choose recovery over pity, choose to stay sober and choose to forget about "Why me?" the tactics that follow can help. Don't worry about the questions, focus on these right answers.

Action Plan

▸ Learn more about the physiology of alcoholism. It may help answer, "Why me?" The more important question is, "What now?"

▸ Practice acceptance. Remember the Serenity Prayer. This is what it's talking about when it says, ". . . accept those things I cannot change."

▸ Follow the old army admonition, "Quit bellyaching'!" Grow up and work on your problem instead of whining about it.

▸ Put up "No Whining!" signs in your living quarters where you can't miss seeing them.

▸ Look around at all those attending your AA meetings. All kinds of people are alcoholics–a lot of them (approximately 10% of the population). You weren't singled out.

- ▸ Review your drinking history and the consequences you've suffered. Notice all the bad choices that *you* have made. Maybe that's "Why you?"
- ▸ Look to the future, instead of dwelling on the past. Have your sponsor help you set recovery goals you can get excited about.
- ▸ Observe other alcoholics who have a "Why me?" attitude. Notice how isolating and self-defeating it is. You can choose to do better.
- ▸ Ask successful and respected recovering alcoholics you know if they worry much about "Why me?" If they say "No" (a safe bet), maybe that's why they're successful and respected.
- ▸ Read inspirational stories about the lives of people who have overcome crippling injuries or life-threatening diseases such as cancer, diabetes or stroke. How many of them were obsessed about "Why me?"
- ▸ Associate with recovering alcoholics who are upbeat and excited about tomorrow. Avoid the "Why me?" whiners. Optimism and hope are contagious.

Trap #65 - "I Give Up."

The worst possible mental state for a recovering alcoholic is an attitude of defeat. If you surrender, there's no place to go. An attitude of "I give up" isn't a wake-up call, it's an alarm!

Occasionally, with or without warning, some

alcoholics decide to give up. They quit caring; they quit trying; they quit believing; they quit feeling–they quit! When this happens, relapse is imminent.

An attitude of "I give up" is an expression of despair. It's a dead-end. It's serious, it's dangerous and it may be fatal. If you begin to harbor thoughts of giving up, you need to take dramatic and immediate action to change your attitude. Your recovery (and your life) may hang in the balance.

When things get this serious, it may take outside assistance to turn your attitude around and to save you from your own negative thinking. Never hesitate to reach out for help when you need it–it seldom will come to you. Seeking help is a sign of strength, not weakness. If you can ask for help, you're not ready to give up yet.

You can find many reasons to give up. Fortunately, there are even more reasons not to. The secret of survival is to recognize your best reasons for staying sober and cling to them–no matter what. Hang on, things will get better. Here are some emergency measures to help you give up on giving up.

Action Plan

▸ Go to church. Meet with your sponsor. Attend AA meetings. These actions should take the highest priority when you're thinking about giving up.
▸ Talk about your feelings. People can't help if they don't know what's going on in your life.
▸ Put off "giving up" until tomorrow.
▸ Consider getting counseling or therapy, returning to treatment or participating in an aftercare program.

You may not be ready to "go it alone" quite yet.

- Pray. This is when you need it most. (See Step 11.)
- List all the reasons you have for hanging in there–be thorough. Include people, things, relationships, unfinished business, future plans and forthcoming events. It's a long list. Why give up now?
- Now, list all the good things about giving up. It's a short list. Why give up now?
- Be with people. This is not a good time to be alone. Besides, it's hard to give up in public.
- Follow the action plan for Trap #41 (Clinical Depression).
- Pamper yourself. (See Appendix E.) Anything you do to lift your spirits gives you reason to pause before giving up.
- In your imagination, let the "spirit of the future" show you what things will be like if you give up now. It may change your mind. It worked for Scrooge. (Mind games can work for you as well as against you.)
- Don't self-medicate to feel better or to get over the urge to give up. Take tranquilizers or other mood-altering drugs only when prescribed by a physician. Be sure the doctor knows you're a recovering alcoholic. You don't need any more addictions to deal with.
- Listen to uplifting music. Sometimes, it's the only voice a desperate person can hear.
- Ask your AA group for feedback. They are the ones who know best why it's crazy to give up–ever.
- Identify one significant thing you want to accomplish before you give up. Do it. Then, identify one more.

A FINAL WORD

Relapse Doesn't Have to Mean Collapse

*Ever tried? Ever failed? No matter. Try again. Fail
again. Fail better."*
Samuel Beckett

Despite conscientious efforts to employ avoidance
techniques and preventive measures, relapse happens.
It's a fact of life. The sobriety-saving action tips
throughout this guide have proved effective in helping
many recovering alcoholics to avert relapse.
Nevertheless, the family, work-related, social, physical,
emotional and attitudinal relapse traps described in
previous pages still snare some well-intentioned sober
alcoholics every day.

If it happens to you, it doesn't have to mean the end.
It means only what you allow it to mean. People get
sober and stay sober in different ways and at their own
pace. Accidents occur. Mistakes are made. Some people
even seem to have to relapse once or twice before they
"get it." For them, relapse is essential to the eventual
recovery. One slip doesn't necessarily make a relapse
and one relapse doesn't necessarily mean the collapse of
your recovery program. You never have to accept relapse
as final.

Likewise, a relapse doesn't prove you're worthless.
It only proves you're human. ("Failure is an event, not a
person." - Zig Ziglar) It's not how many times you slip
that counts, it's how many times you get back up.

If you suffer a relapse, learn something. (Relapse can
be a good teacher.) Then, try again. Redouble your

169

efforts to avoid everyday elapse traps by using the action plans in this book. This may be the time you make it for good.

Recovery is forever. Recovery expert, Terence Gorski, reminds us, "The disease is called alcoholi-*ism*, not alcohol-*wasm*." The disease won't quit. You shouldn't either.

A relapse may be just another chapter in your recovery or it may be the conclusion. You are the only author of your life's story. You can write-in sobriety and serenity as the final entry. What a climax!

You deserve a happy ending as much as anyone. Why not start living yours today?

The End

APPENDIXES

Appendix A

WARNING SIGNS

Signals a Relapse is On the Way

Relapse doesn't happen unannounced. Almost always, certain attitudes and behaviors serve as red flags signaling a relapse on the way.

By themselves, no one of these signals is particularly alarming. However, when they occur in combinations and persist over time, they constitute a warning that shouldn't be ignored.

Backsliding is reversible and relapse is preventable. You can stave off a ruinous relapse if corrective actions are taken as soon as telltale signs begin to creep into your everyday behavior. The trick is to monitor your actions and emotions and act on what you learn. Enlisting family can be useful, friends and supporters to help in spotting trouble-in-the-making. Here's what to look out for:

- Dreams about drinking
- Rapid mood swings
- Boredom
- Self-pity
- Unexplained fatigue
- Changes in eating/sleeping habits
- Loneliness
- Immature (childish) behavior

- Vague feelings of dissatisfaction
- Forgetfulness
- Interest in controlled usage
- Increased cravings
- Lethargy
- Increase in painful flashbacks and withdrawal memories
- Nervousness
- Excessive daydreaming
- Defensiveness
- Paranoia
- Confusion
- Irritability
- Guilt feelings
- Pessimism
- Loss of sense of humor
- Negative feelings
- Fixation on euphoric recall
- Jealousy directed toward drinkers
- Increasing need to test yourself
- Anger
- Shame
- Giving in to other compulsive behaviors
- Sense of damnation (Alienation from God)
- Cease planning and goal-setting
- Crazy feelings which are hard to control
- Feeling stressed out

- Feelings of inferiority
- Sleeplessness
- Rejection of help
- Obsession (Tunnel Vision)
- Changes in habits and routines
- Resentment
- Irritability
- Confusion
- Denial
- Stop going to AA meetings
- Avoidance of sponsor and AA friends
- Blaming
- Depression
- Epidemic of poor choices and bad judgment
- Withdrawal from social contacts
- Binge eating
- Skipping or rushing meals
- "I'm cured" attitude
- Argumentativeness
- Putting the 12 Steps on the back burner
- Mounting debts and money problems
- Secret thoughts about drinking
- Becoming accident prone
- Feeling hopeless and helpless
- Abusing cigarettes and coffee
- "Awfulizing" sobriety (Being dry is terrible)
- "Catastrophizing" (a worse case scenario)

Appendix B

HOW TO SAY "NO"
How to Turn Down a Drink
and Make it Stick

Just saying "No" to alcohol isn't as easy as it may seem. "No" is a simple word. You use it hundreds of times a year, but when you're a newcomer to sobriety and have to turn down a drink in front of old cronies and others who have known you as a user, it's the hardest word in the language to say.

Being able to speak up and speak out to refuse a drink is one of recovery's first tests. It's not easy. It can stir up unwanted feelings of self-consciousness, vulnerability, inadequacy, weakness and embarrassment. It takes guts to say "No" the first time. Some "wannabe" recovering alcoholics can't handle it and cave in. It's foolish to risk relapse over a single word, but it happens.

Veteran AA members, who recall the fragility of early sobriety, advise planning and rehearsing refusal phrases before the time you will need to use them. Practicing turn-down phrases ahead of time has helped many recovering alcoholics to feel more comfortable and confident in sensitive social situations. It can work for you too.

Many ways are available for saying "No." A list of frequently used, ready-made refusal phrases are below. Take your pick. Don't let a few words stand between you and your sobriety.

- ✔ I'm fine for now.
- ✔ My doctor doesn't want me to drink.
- ✔ I'm allergic to alcohol.
- ✔ I'm the designated driver.
- ✔ No, thanks.
- ✔ I'm on a diet.
- ✔ I don't feel like drinking right now.
- ✔ I don't have time for a drink.
- ✔ What else do you have?
- ✔ Maybe later.
- ✔ I've had my quota.
- ✔ My stomach won't take it.
- ✔ No more for me.
- ✔ Not now.
- ✔ I've got to keep a clear head for a meeting later.
- ✔ I'm not in the mood.
- ✔ I have a craving for iced tea, soda, or juice.
- ✔ My horoscope says not to drink today.
- ✔ Let my friend have my share.
- ✔ I'll wait awhile.
- ✔ I'm trying to cut down.
- ✔ Booze isn't good for my ulcer.
- ✔ I couldn't drink another drop.
- ✔ Nothing for me.
- ✔ I'm already high on sugar.
- ✔ I gave up alcohol for Lent.
- ✔ Somebody's got to stay sober to keep this crowd

out of trouble.

- ✔ This soda tastes good to me tonight.
- ✔ I can't decide. You'd better move on.
- ✔ I don't want to drink and drive.
- ✔ I've decided not to drink for a while.
- ✔ I've had enough to last me for a long time.
- ✔ I want to be able to taste my food.
- ✔ This isn't my night to drink.
- ✔ That iced tea looks good to me.
- ✔ I'll pass for now.
- ✔ Booze and I don't get along.
- ✔ I'm on duty. I can't drink now.
- ✔ I never drink before dinner.
- ✔ I need a coffee fix.
- ✔ I'm not supposed to eat or drink anything for 12 hours.
- ✔ Just water. I'm really thirsty.
- ✔ Let me think awhile. I'll let you know if I want something.
- ✔ I've had enough.
- ✔ I have a headache.
- ✔ I'm not drinking right now.
- ✔ I don't want to smell like liquor.
- ✔ I don't want to get sleepy.
- ✔ Booze doesn't taste good to me right now.
- ✔ I'm in a hurry. I'm ready to order my meal now.
- ✔ I'll say "No" for now.

- ✔ I can't mix alcohol with the medication I'm taking.
- ✔ I'll hold off for a while.
- ✔ I don't want anything to drink.
- ✔ I'M AN ALCOHOLIC
- ✔ No!

Appendix C

ALCOHOL-FREE FUN

How to Have a Life and Enjoy it Without Drinking

When drunks first get sober, they often don't know how to have fun without alcohol. It's scary. Many fear they will never be able to enjoy life or have a good time again. Fortunately, their fears are unfounded–there is fun after sobriety!

Your fun after you quit drinking will be better because you will be fully aware of what is going on and you will remember it all the next morning.

Below is a sampler of activities which are low cost, family-friendly, fun-filled and alcohol-free. The list is illustrative, not exhaustive. If you need additional ideas, check Appendix E (Personal Pampering).

With these starter-suggestions, your creativity and imagination can easily whip up more fun than you can handle. Who needs alcohol? Enjoy!

❖ Play cards.

❖ Read. Read aloud. Read to each other.

❖ Go fishing.

❖ Cook your favorite food.

❖ Take nature walks.

❖ Work out.

❖ Call on old friends.

❖ Make travel or vacation plans.

- ✤ Take in a movie or play.
- ✤ Go bowling.
- ✤ Visit an art gallery.
- ✤ Play miniature golf.
- ✤ Try new restaurants.
- ✤ Work a jigsaw puzzle.
- ✤ Go on a picnic.
- ✤ Learn something new.
- ✤ Work on your car.
- ✤ Play your favorite sports.
- ✤ Write for pleasure.
- ✤ Attend concerts.
- ✤ Work in your garden.
- ✤ Go camping.
- ✤ Hunt for seashells.
- ✤ Fly a kite.
- ✤ Star gaze.
- ✤ Ride a merry-go-round.
- ✤ Join a singing group.
- ✤ Learn to whistle (or yodel).
- ✤ Visit a museum.
- ✤ Watch favorite TV reruns.
- ✤ Go on a hayride.
- ✤ Make homemade ice cream.
- ✤ Enjoy fall foliage.
- ✤ Read a magazine.
- ✤ Create something.

- ✥ Go to a circus or a carnival.
- ✥ Play a pick up game of hoops, volleyball or touch football.
- ✥ Walk in the rain.
- ✥ Play in the leaves or play in the snow.
- ✥ Bake cookies.
- ✥ Enjoy a romantic, candlelight dinner.
- ✥ Build model airplanes.
- ✥ Go to the beach.
- ✥ Gamble (if you can do it just for fun).
- ✥ Start a collection.
- ✥ People watch.
- ✥ Take up a new hobby.
- ✥ Find a theater still showing the Rocky Horror Picture Show.
- ✥ Visit a zoo.
- ✥ Go to a comedy club.
- ✥ Rent a video.
- ✥ Shoot pool.
- ✥ Learn some magic tricks.
- ✥ Do something for others.

Add your favorite things to do without booze

- ✥ . . . .

- ✥ . . . .

- ✥ . . . .

❖ . . . .

❖ . . . .

❖ . . . .

❖ . . . .

Let the (sober) good times roll!

Appendix D

POSITIVE SELF-TALK

Self Affirmations
To Help Prevent Relapse

You have self esteem problems if you're like most drunks. Feelings of inadequacy often form the foundation for alcoholism, and so many alcoholics try to find courage and confidence in a bottle. It doesn't work. Recovery depends on reclaiming a positive vision of your self worth.

Staying sober starts in the mind. If you believe you can make it, you will. A lot depends on the messages you give yourself. A big part of beating alcohol is convincing yourself that you can be saved and you're worth saving.

One way to do this is to feed yourself positive self talk. Many successful performers in all fields start each day by reciting self-affirming mental messages. Self-affirmations are an effective stay-sober tool for recovering alcoholics as well. It may seem silly at first, but it makes a difference. It's a way to boost self-confidence, validate your self worth, avoid relapse traps and prepare yourself to face another day without alcohol.

If you haven't tried positive self-talk as an aid to sobriety, you're missing a good bet. Why not be your own best cheerleader?

When you're serious about sobriety, you'll take any

help you can get. Try repeating the following self-affirming statements each morning. They're easy, they're free and they work. Good luck!

- ✌ I know I can do it.
- ✌ I can do it one day at a time.
- ✌ I am enough.
- ✌ I can stop drinking.
- ✌ I like being sober.
- ✌ My cravings are decreasing every day. I can outlast any craving.
- ✌ I don't need alcohol to have fun.
- ✌ My life is better without alcohol.
- ✌ I won't drink today.
- ✌ I'm okay.
- ✌ God won't give me more than I can handle.
- ✌ People love me. They don't want me to drink.
- ✌ I can do whatever it takes to stay sober.
- ✌ I'm too smart to make myself stupid with alcohol.
- ✌ I feel better every day I don't drink.
- ✌ My family will respect me again.
- ✌ It's a challenge I can master.
- ✌ I'm getting wiser.
- ✌ I have the power to stop.
- ✌ I can stay sober even when I'm tired, scared, angry, sad or excited.
- ✌ I'm an adult.
- ✌ I know what's right. I can do the right thing.
- ✌ I don't need anyone to tell me what to do or think.

- I can manage stress without booze.
- I'm making a better life for myself.
- I have the tools to stay sober.
- I believe in myself and in my ability to beat alcohol.
- I'm strong enough to keep from drinking.
- God isn't done with me yet. He has plans for me that don't include alcohol.
- People will help me stay sober.
- I can learn to quit drinking.
- I owe it to myself.
- My child wants to be just like me.
- This ending is just the beginning.
- I'm mature enough to make healthy choices.
- Lots of people like me. I don't need alcohol to have friends.
- I am prepared to deal with any situation that might tempt me to drink.
- I have a plan to avoid relapse.
- Drinking makes me sick. I want to be healthy.
- I choose not to take that first drink.
- The urge to drink will pass whether I drink or not.
- I have a Higher Power.
- One drink *does* matter.
- I am responsible for my sobriety.
- I can make new friends.
- I have a right to say "No."

- ✌ I can accept that I can't drink.
- ✌ Real friends don't pressure friends to drink.
- ✌ I'm staying sober for myself.
- ✌ I don't need booze.
- ✌ Today is the first day of the rest of my sobriety.
- ✌ I am a better person without alcohol.
- ✌ It's my choice. I choose not to drink.
- ✌ I can accomplish anything one day at a time.
- ✌ I am taking back my life.
- ✌ My body is too precious to poison with alcohol.
- ✌ I look better, feel better, even smell better without booze.
- ✌ Staying sober is the most important thing I have to do today.
- ✌ I want to be a good role model.
- ✌ I'm tired of drinking and tired of lying.
- ✌ I'll feel great about myself.
- ✌ I plan to celebrate my 100th birthday.
- ✌ Nothing and no one controls me.
- ✌ The long-range benefits of sobriety easily outweigh any short-term discomfort.
- ✌ I have no problems that booze can make better.
- ✌ My Higher Power will help me.
- ✌ I can manage my emotions without alcohol.
- ✌ People depend on me. I won't let them down.
- ✌ I have important things yet to do.
- ✌ I am a unique human being.

- I have a disease; but I don't have to die from it.
- God doesn't want me to drink.
- I am free. I won't be a slave to alcohol.
- I can help others. I can make the world a better place.
- I'm glad I'm sober.
- I have it in me to live a sober life.
- I remember the consequences of drinking. I don't want to go there again.
- I want to live.
- Whatever it takes to stay sober, I'm worth it.
- I'm working on my shortcomings. I'm becoming a better person.
- I have a lot to offer.
- I accept myself, so I can accept others.
- When I look in the mirror, I like what I see.
- It's never too late to quit.
- There's no time like now.
- The other times were for practice.
- For me, the best is yet to come.
- I'm going to surprise the whole world.
- I am a miracle!

Appendix E

PERSONAL PAMPERING

Ways to Reward Yourself for Averting a Relapse

Recovery is incremental. It builds day by day through a series of small successes. The key to continued progress is to celebrate each victory. You owe yourself a reward for passing each day's sobriety tests and avoiding relapse traps along the way.

Sobriety isn't easy. Relish each hard-won success. Pamper yourself: give yourself a prize. If you don't, who will?

Below are ways recovering alcoholics frequently reward themselves for staying sober, working the 12-Steps and rebuilding a productive life. Pick what works for you or invent your own rewards. It doesn't have to be something big, just enjoyable for you. Only you know what makes you feel special. Do it–you deserve it. You'll be glad you did.

☺ Eat chocolate.

☺ Sleep late.

☺ Buy some new shoes.

☺ Get a massage.

☺ Watch a sunset.

☺ Smoke a good cigar.

☺ Ride in a limousine.

☺ Buy that trinket (jewelry) you've been putting off getting for yourself.

☺ Splurge on concert tickets.

☺ Eat pizza for breakfast.

☺ Send yourself a bouquet.

☺ Get a manicure or a pedicure.

☺ Stay up late to watch a favorite old movie.

☺ Enjoy a weekend getaway at a picturesque bed and breakfast.

☺ Eat all you want of whatever you want.

☺ Enjoy a leisurely bubble bath.

☺ Try a new hair style.

☺ Dress casually even though it's not Friday.

☺ Have breakfast in bed.

☺ Hire a cleaning person.

☺ Go to a ball game.

☺ Buy some sexy underwear.

☺ Add something to your collection.

☺ Romp with your dog. (You'll both have a good time.)

☺ Order lobster.

☺ Take time out to go to a driving range–or a shooting range.

☺ Get a facial.

☺ Read a trashy novel.

☺ Cancel your dentist's appointment and do something fun instead.

☺ Go first class.

☺ Forget your diet and order a double-malted.

☺ Take a hot air balloon ride.

☺ Lie in the sun.

☺ Go power shopping.

☺ Try a new cologne or aftershave.

☺ Call your best out-of-town friend.

☺ Go wading in the surf.

☺ Play hooky from a boring business meeting.

☺ Eat ice cream out of the carton.

☺ Buy a special tool or piece of equipment.

☺ Listen to a favorite record or CD.

☺ Try bungy jumping.

☺ Wiggle your toes in the mud.

☺ Buy a copy of *Playboy* (or *Playgirl*). Read it and look at all the pictures without feeling guilty.

☺ Have lunch with a friend (not an old drinking buddy).

☺ Build a fire. Toast marshmallows.

☺ Take a hot shower for as long as you want.

☺ Get that software you've been eyeing.

☺ Go for a drive.

☺ Work a crossword puzzle.

☺ Get dressed up and strut around the mall (or get undressed and strut around at home).

☺ Make popcorn.

☺ Get a make-over.

- ☺ Sip a cup of herbal tea.
- ☺ Enjoy some "quiet time."
- ☺ Let Glamour Shots make a fashion photo portrait of you looking your best.
- ☺ Take a cooking class.
- ☺ Buy a new fishing lure, pair of running shoes or designer golf balls.
- ☺ Spend a day at your favorite place.
- ☺ Enjoy a special coffee latté or mocha.
- ☺ Serve dinner using your finest china and best silver.
- ☺ Let someone else mow the lawn.
- ☺ Buy a computer game.
- ☺ Don't set the alarm clock.
- ☺ Walk, don't run, through your favorite park. Take time to smell the roses and feed the geese.
- ☺ Spend some extra time on your hobby.
- ☺ Chew bubble gum and blow bubbles as you did when you were a kid.

Your Favorite Rewards

☺ . . . .

☺ . . . .

☺ . . . .

☺ . . . .

☺ . . . .

☺ . . . .

☺ . . . .

☺ . . . .

☺ . . . .

☺ . . . .

☺ . . . .

Appendix F

THE 12-STEPS
OF ALCOHOLICS ANONYMOUS

1. We admitted we were powerless over alcohol–that our lives had become unmanageable.

2. Came to believe that a Power greater than ourselves could restore us to sanity.

3. Made a decision to turn our will and our lives over to the care of God as we understood Him.

4. Made a searching and fearless moral inventory of ourselves.

5. Admitted to God, to ourselves and to another human being the exact nature of our wrongs.

6. Were entirely ready to have God remove all of these defects of character.

7. Humbly asked Him to remove our shortcomings.

8. Made a list of all persons we had harmed and became willing to make amends to them all.

9. Made direct amends to such people wherever possible except when to do so would injure them or others.

10. Continued to take personal inventory and when we were wrong, promptly admitted it.

11. Sought through prayer and meditation to improve our conscious contact with God as we understood Him, praying only for knowledge of His will for us and the power to carry that out.

12. Having had a spiritual awakening as the result of these Steps, we tried to carry this message to alcoholics, and to practice these principles in all our affairs.

Appendix G

The Serenity Prayer

God,
grant me the serenity
To accept
the things I cannot change,
Courage
to change the things I can,
And wisdom
to know the difference.

A RELAPSE-PREVENTION READING LIST

Reading is a basic source of information and information is a basic source of power. It's no wonder, then, that millions of recovering alcoholics read self-help and inspirational literature on a regular basis. It's another way to gain power and control over alcohol.

Curling up with a good book or pamphlet may seem like a "cushy" way to stay sober, but it works. That's why reading should become an important part of your daily recovery program.

Many publications are available about recovery. However, even though relapse is a universal fear and a common experience among alcoholics, relatively few good materials specifically on relapse are available. Some of the best are listed below.

If you need more help, tap these readings for the information and the power they have to offer. Why not start today?

Crewe, Charles. *A Look at Relapse* (pamphlet), Center City, MN: Hazelden 1996

Cusak, Suzanne Boylston. *Women and Relapse* (pamphlet), Center City, MN: Hazelden, 1996

Daley, Dennis D. *Preventing Relapse Workbook*, Center City, MN: Hazelden, 1996

Dunn, Richard. *Relapse and the Addict*, Center City, MN: Hazelden, 1986

Evans and Sullivan. *Preventing Relapse* (pamphlet), Center City, MN: Hazelden, 1991

Free-Gardiner, Linda. *Trust the Process: How to Enhance Recovery and Prevent Relapse*, Ventura, CA: Newjoy Press, 1996

Free-Gardiner, Linda. *Trust the Process: How to Enhance Recovery and Prevent Relapse Workbook*, Ventura, CA: Newjoy Press, 1996

Gorski, Terence T. *The Relapse Recovery Grid*, (booklet), Center City, MN: Hazelden, 1989

Gorski, Terence T and Miller, Merlene. *Mistaken Beliefs about Relapse*, Center City, MN: Hazelden, 1984

Gorski, Terence T. and Miller, Merlene. *Staying Sober*, Center City, MN: Hazeldon, 1987. (Accompanying workbook available. Published 1992

Nuckols, Cardwell. *Roadblocks to Recovery*, Center City, MN: Hazelden, 1996

Swanson, Jan, and Cooper, Alan. *Coping with Emotional and Physical High-risk Factors* (The Complete Relapse Prevention Skills Program Series), Center City, MN: Hazelden, 1994

Swanson, Jan and Cooper, Alan. *Coping with Personal and Social High-Risk Factors* (The Complete Relapse Prevention Skills Program Series), Center City, MN: Hazelden, 1994

Swanson, Jan and Cooper, Alan. *Identifying Your High-risk Factors* (The Complete Relapse Prevention Skills

Program Series), Center City, MN: Hazelden, 1994

W, Anne. *Now What Do I Do for Fun?* (pamphlet), Center City, MN: Hazelden, 1996

Ward, Robert. *When You Go to Work* (pamphlet), Center City, MN: Hazelden, 1996

Order Form

Please send me the following:

Amt.	Item	Each	Total
	Relapse Traps	$15.95	
	Trust the Process	$15.95	
	Trust the Process Workbook	$15.95	
Postage & Handling 1 book $1.80 Each additional book add 25 cents Orders of 10 or more books/workbooks will be invoiced separately.		Subtotal	
		*Tax	
		P&H	
Priority , UPS, Overnight mail for extra fee		TOTAL	

California residents pay 7.25% sales tax

√ **Mail this form with check or credit card information**
√ **Call: 800-876-1373**
√ **Fax: 805-984-0503**

Card No.__ __ __ __ __ __ __ __ __ __ __ __ __ __ __ __

Signature_____Exp. Date_____

☐ Visa   ☐ MasterCard   ☐ American Express   ☐ Check

Please print clearly

Name_____

Address_____

City, State, Zip_____

Phone(_____)_____

Newjoy Press, P.O. Box 3437, Ventura, CA 93006

Unconditional Guarantee
If you are not satisfied with your purchase, return it for a full refund.

Thank you for your order